HIGH PROTEIN VEGAN MEAL PREP COOKBOOK

Super Easy 28-day meal plan with feel-good, plant-based diet recipes &
nutrition guide for ultimate fitness, bodybuilding and rapid weight loss

BENJAMIN REEVES

Feelight Publishing

CONTENTS

WEEK 1

WEEK 1 RECIPES

WEEK 2

WEEK 3

WEEK 4

"EAT WHAT NOURISHES YOUR *Body*
AND DO WHAT NOURISHES YOUR *Soul*."

INTRODUCTION

Hi! Nice to see you here, fellow vegan!

Maybe you're still transitioning from vegetarian or even omnivore, but that's okay. We all make our own decisions, but I want to let you know that becoming vegan is one of the best decisions we've ever made in our lives.

When Trisha and I first started eating plant-based/vegan, the first challenge we faced was the lack of time to meal prep. We spent hours and hours in the kitchen, just to make sure we prepared the most healthy and tasty meals for our us and our daughter, but as a result, we didn't have so much time to be working out our simply spending quality time together.

Before going plant-based, Trisha, my wife was already a vegetarian and I was still an omnivore, but after going plant-based for our daughter and feeling amazing, we started looking for ways to save time on cooking and still be able to have yummy home-cooked meals ready at all times - and that was when we discovered this powerful tool: meal prepping.

Our goals have always been to educate, inspire and empower people to take control of their health, and the first step is actually to start with what you eat.

We've seen hundreds of people transformed with our healthy home-cooked vegan recipes, improved their health and also gained confidence. That's the reason why we knew we had to share our new meal prep method and meal plan with more people.

I know that for you, as a vegan or vegetarian, it is oftentimes hard to plan every single meal in advance and know exactly what to buy each week in the grocery store. It is also a common struggle for new vegetarians or vegans to know what type of foods are high in protein and thus good for your health. I've seen so many new vegans only eating carbohydrate dense food, which is not ideal for gaining muscle, losing fat or boosting your metabolism.

That's why we've put in the effort to design a meal plan that's healthy, delicious and good for you and your family at the same time.

What this book offers is a way to plan your meals on a dish by dish basis so you make the most of every opportunity to lose fat, gain muscle and maintain your health. Alongside using this meal plan, we advise that you have a carefully prepared exercise regimen. This will enable the meal plan to be a more helpful guide to assist your fitness journey.

We have designed this book of recipes to be your constant companion, taking you day by day through your fitness journey. This book exists to give you nutritious yet tasty meals that will help you to meet your goals and leave you feeling energetic and ready for whatever life has to throw at you. If you have been concerned that a vegan diet will leave you feeling run down and tired, then you have nothing to fear here. All of these recipes have been created and optimized to be the solution that you need to realize your dreams.

Before we dive in to the meal plans and recipes, allow me to tell you a little bit about myself. My name is Benjamin Reeves, and I have been a professional personal trainer since I was in my early twenties. I have helped hundreds of people achieve their nutrition and fitness goals since then.

I am now in my thirties and my wife, Trisha, and I are expecting our second child. It is this anticipation that drove me to put together all my best vegan recipes into an easy meal prep guide that shows you how to batch cook and prep your meals in one day giving you more time over the week to focus on your training and work and other commitments. After all, it's better to enjoy our time with our family, friends and loved ones rather than spending hours everyday in the kitchen, right?

WHAT YOU WILL DISCOVER IN THIS BOOK - HIGH PROTEIN VEGAN MEAL PREP MADE SIMPLE!

In this book, you will find recipes that have been designed to be relatively higher in protein and lower in carbohydrate, and therefore are great for losing fat and gaining muscles. It is especially important for vegans or vegetarians to pay attention to their protein intake.

Each week, you will find 1 weekly meal plan (it's a 6-day meal plan, allowing you some space to enjoy eating out with friends, or to simply have a cheat day), 1 meal prep guide, 1 shopping list, as well as the recipes for the week.

If you stick to this meal plan (which is actually quite easy because all the shopping list and macros have been done for you), and exercise at least 3 times per week, I am confident that you will see some great results after 28 days.

But first, you have to ask yourself: what is your main fitness and nutrition goal? Do you want to lose fat? Gain muscles? Or do you want to simply feel amazing? It is really important that you define your goal and actually write it down. Next, you need to know where you are today. Take your measurements now, and then write down the numbers, and take them again after this month. I'm also a big believer in progress pictures. If you have a big mirror at home, you might want to start taking progress pictures daily. At the end of the day, what's most important is how you look, and not your weight. Sometimes people get frustrated to see their weight increases, but you have to realize that muscles are a lot heavier than fat, and therefore you might gain weight but look more fit than ever. So my advice is to pay more attention to how you look in the mirror than your weight. You will be surprised when people start commenting on how amazing you look after you stick to this habit of taking progress pictures, providing that you're eating healthy and exercising regularly.

Lastly, I would like to ask you to get enough sleep daily. Sleeping for 7-9 hours per night is crucial, especially if you are looking to change body composition, increase muscle mass and/or if you want to be ready for your training session the next day. Sleep enhances muscle recovery through protein synthesis and human growth hormone release, and thus it is crucial for your success.

My book is only a tool that will help you get the body and health you've wanted for so long, but in the end, you are the one who has to put in the effort here. With enough determination and discipline, I believe that you will achieve your ultimate fitness goals sooner than you think.

Take this book of recipes and make it yours. Make it your constant companion on your journey to your ultimate destination, a stronger, healthier, happier you!

"A healthy outside starts from the inside."

-Robert Urich

WHAT DOES A HIGH PROTEIN, PLANT-BASED DIET LOOK LIKE?

Benefits of a high protein plant-based diet

I believe that if you're reading this book, chances are you are already aware of the benefits of a plant-based diet, but I will still discuss them briefly just so we are all on the same page. In a plant-based diet, you only eat vegetables, fruits, beans, lentils, and all non-animal food products. The popularity of this diet has been rising over the last decades, and countless studies have proven the many benefits that this diet can provide. You might be adopting this lifestyle for moral or environmental reasons, however, many vegans and vegetarians follow the diet specifically to gain the benefits that this diet provides. Being a plant-based dieter means that you are aware of different problems and are willing to step up to solve them. Some advantages are:

BOOSTING IMMUNITY:

Vegetables and fruits have lots of micronutrients that give a helping hand to our immune system. Antioxidants in berries, phytochemicals in vegetables, and many different minerals and vitamins collectively help prevent infections.

PREVENTING CANCER:

The diet has gone through extensive studies and has been proven to reduce the chances of many different types of cancers. This is mainly due to eating less processed foods with toxins in them and consuming more antioxidants.

HELPING IN WEIGHT LOSS:

Whole foods, vegetables, and other plant-based natural products have one thing in common – they are high in fiber. This keeps blood sugar controlled, belly full, and leaves almost no extra carbohydrates or calories for the body to store.

SAVING THE ENVIRONMENT:

Just by cutting out meat and meat-based products from your life reduces your carbon emission footprint by almost 75%. Collectively and with time, this reduces water and land use, deforestation, and pollution:

By following a high protein plant-based diet, you will get all the above benefits. However, the increasing protein will help you in many other ways as well. When incorporating exercise and muscle building in your daily life, eating a high protein plant-based diet could really benefit your training.

YOU CAN BUILD MUSCLE WITHOUT EXCESS FAT OR CARBS:

The basics of muscle building is to consume just enough food to burn in your exercise and workout session. Muscle growth and repair all hinges on how much protein you are consuming. Plant-based foods are less calorie dense than meat and other animal products due to the water content of fruits and vegetables. This means you can maintain a steady quantity of calories, reach your macronutrient goals but also head to the gym not feeling hungry.

THEY PROVIDE ENOUGH PROTEIN:

In developed countries, the main sources of protein come from meat and dairy. We can't call a dish a full meal without some sort of "protein." Look at other countries that don't use animal meat as the primary source of protein. They use lentils, tofu, beans, nuts, and seeds. We don't eat these kinds of food here that often. That's why there is a general perception of plant foods being low in protein. People who are non-plant-based eaters, while consuming meat, have to adjust their diet. They eat more to get sufficient protein, but they also end up gaining a lot of fats in their meals.

IT BOOSTS PERFORMANCE AND RECOVERY:

Many athletes around the world are leaving meat for this reason. Numerous studies show many ways why this occurs. It reduces inflammation in their body by cutting processed foods and adding antioxidants, polyphenols, and fiber. A plant-based diet is good for healthy gut microbes. They help in reducing inflammation and oxidative stress, which in turn helps with a nice exercise routine.

This book will provide you the information you need to gain muscle in a plant-based diet. Every week's meal plan is high in protein and has a wide range of different vegetables and other ingredients to also provide you with a good selection of minerals, vitamins, and micronutrients.

MACRONUTRIENTS AND MICRONUTRIENTS

Calories are the amount of energy that a food contains. All types of food and ingredients are made up of nutrients and divided into two groups – macronutrients, and micronutrients. Macronutrients are consumed in high amounts as carbohydrates, fats, and protein. Micronutrients are consumed in lower quantities as different minerals and vitamins.

A healthy diet consists of a diverse food source. This ensures that you are getting all the micronutrients, minerals, and vitamins that you need. These micronutrients have many functions, increasing immunity, developing the brain, growth, absorption, and many other specific roles that only they can do. Not consuming them or eating them in excess will lead you to nutritional diseases. A diverse diet will ensure that your body's known and even unknown needs are being fulfilled.

Most fitness goals center around calorie counting and macronutrients, but not much attention is given to the latter. Even if you have no interest in fitness goals, you have likely heard of being aware of calories when on a diet. Calorie counting has become so popular that it has cast a shadow on the nutritional value of food; this value can give us information that calories don't.

Nutritional information tell us whether the food is healthy or not:

200 calories of candy are not equal to 200 calories of vegetables. The calories coming from candy will most likely be stored and lead to weight gain, while the calories coming from veggies will be burned and used up. The nutrient levels of vegetables and sweets are not the same, even if their calories are.

Nutritional information tells you the whole picture and what the food is made up of:

Calorie counting will not give you the full picture. Reading macronutrients and micronutrients of food will provide you with a better understanding of what healthy and unhealthy foods are made up of. You'll get a better understanding of what to and not to eat.

Nutritional information helps in designing a better fitness diet plan:

People who want to lose weight, who want to build-up muscles, or who want to do both will have to consume different proportions of the macronutrients compared to someone who is looking to gain weight for example. Calories counting may help in adjusting your weight but in order to build muscle and make gains in the gym, a suitable diet plan focused on a suitable macronutrient profile will be more effective in helping you reach your desired goals.

INGREDIENTS LIST IMPORTANCE

Not every food is created equal, and not every plant-based food has the same amount of macronutrients. There are plenty of fatty foods out there like vegetable oils. We are not going to be eating them for this diet. We need a specific amount of macronutrients that can only come from a carefully concocted list.

Many veggies, fruits, and other plant-based food products are high in carbs. In a weight loss diet, you need to consume low carb fruits and vegetables. Also, you are focused on muscle gain as well. You need to focus more on eating foods that will provide you with the most protein, the macronutrient that will build muscles. For your goal, an ingredient list of low carbs and high protein is necessary. If you want to create recipes on your own in the future, you can use the ingredients from this list to facilitate your diet.

THE HIGH PROTEIN, PLANT-BASED INGREDIENT LIST

Plant-based
HIGH PROTEIN
Ingredients

Protein per 100g

Peanut Butter	23g
Tahini (sesame seed paste)	22g
Tempeh	19g
Rolled Wholegrain Oats	19g
Pumpkin Seeds	17g
Chia Seed or Flaxseed	16g-18g
Nuts (cashews, walnuts, hazelnuts, pistachio, etc.)	15g-20g
Tofu	15g
Quinoa	14g
Buckwheat	13g
Edamame Beans	11g
Cooked Beans (chickpea, kidney, black, adzuki, etc.)	9g
Cooked Lentils (all varieties)	9g
Green Peas	5g
Soy Milk	3.3g
Brown Rice	3g
Spinach	3g
Sweet Corn	3g
Broccoli	2.8g
Coconut Milk (full-fat)	2.3g
Asparagus	2.2g
Potatoes	2g
Sweet Potatoes	1.6g

WHAT ARE LOW CARB VEGETABLES AND FRUITS? WHAT ARE NET CARBS?

Fruits and vegetables are, most of the time, low in calories and fat—one of the main reasons why people like eating them for losing weight. But if you also want to cut carbs, you need to choose cautiously.

Fruits have sugar in them, some diets limit their usage, but the sugar from them isn't that bad. They can serve a good purpose in sufficient amounts. Many fruits have low carbs because they are mostly filled with water and fiber. Because they have higher fiber, they have less absorbable carbs.

Absorbable carbs are carbs that will enter your bloodstream and alter blood sugar levels. This type of carb is known as net carbs. Fiber is also a type of carbohydrates, but this kind of carb doesn't enter the bloodstream and doesn't alter sugar levels. To find out how many net carbs there are in a food product, you have to subtract the amount of fiber from total carbs.

LOW CARB FRUITS AND VEGETABLES

Low-Carb
FRUITS & VEGETABLES
Net Carbs per 100g

Romaine Lettuce	1.2g
Celery	1.4g
Avocado	2g
Aubergine/Eggplant	2g
Cabbage	2.2g
Mushrooms	2.2g
Kale	2.7g
Cauliflower	3g
Olives	3g
Courgette/Zucchini	3g
Bell Peppers (yellow, orange, red)	3g
Cucumber	3g
Tomatoes	3.1g
Pumpkin	3.3g
Berries (strawberries, blackberries, raspberries)	4g-6g
Squash	5g
Green Bell Peppers	6g
Coconut	6.3g
Fennel	7g
Melons (watermelon, cantouple etc)	7g-8g
Grapefruit, Lemons or Limes	7g-9g
Onions	7.3g
Carrots	9g
Blueberries	9g
Peaches, Nectarines, Plums	8g-10g
Beetroot	10g
Potatoes	14.8g
Sweet Potato	17g

TIPS & TRICKS FOR HIGH-PROTEIN VEGAN MEAL PREPPING

Meal prep doesn't just mean to buy all the ingredients; it also means to organize and fill up your kitchen with useful tools to allow you to be efficient when creating and storing your meals for the week. Having a kitchen set up for your diet will make it easy for you to follow the diet according to the plan. It will make life much more straightforward.

No matter if you're a meal prep pro or new to the trend, a perfect kitchen set-up will make life a little more bearable. Cooking with plants isn't that difficult; you get accustomed to using different ingredients. Cooking techniques and having the right tools ready and placed conveniently on the shelves will help you a lot.

Having a well-stocked kitchen means you can cook quickly, without much fuss and irritation. You will have fun cooking and playing around with ingredients to make your creations. This book is a guide for people wanting maximum efficiency. Design your kitchen for success today by using the following tips and tricks.

Suggestions for extra kitchen tools for meal preparation day:

CHOPPER/ADJUSTABLE SLICER

This tool is beneficial when you are primarily eating vegetables. These tools allow you to have precise cuts in a few minutes rather than spending hours on a chopping board. Vegetables need slicing, and they are an efficient, fast, and effective way to do it. A variety of cuts can be made by adjusting the slicer. You can dice, julienne, cut, or grate. The tool's importance in my kitchen is immense.

SPIRALIZER

This is an innovative gadget that transforms the shape of doughs, veggies, fruits, etc.; into noodles. Only the shape changes, so you have creative ways to use and eat different food to your liking. The spiralizer can turn your plant-based food into fettuccine, ribbon, spaghetti, etc. You can set the desired texture and consistency as well. This machine can make dieting and cooking fun.

FOOD PROCESSOR

People often get the functions of blenders and food processors confused. The former blends the ingredients until their liquid, while the processor mixes the food particles in a chunkier manner. Food Processors are perfect for making chunky sauces such as hummus or pesto and can offer a quick solution to making cauliflower rice or your own nut butters.

KNIFE SET

One of the most vital tools in the kitchen of a home and professional chef is a knife. A good set of knives can make cutting vegetables, dicing herbs, and cutting thick fruits like melons and squash a lot easier.

HIGH-SPEED BLENDER

A blender has many uses in a plant-based kitchen. It can be used to make smoothies, batters, sauces and soups. Having a high-quality, high-speed blender will create a smoother texture compared to a more low-budget model. Cheaper models are still great to have if other models are not within your price range, it might just take longer for you to fully blend your sauces and smoothies.

GRATER

All of us have used this tool for grating cheese for pizza or a salad. What if I tell you that you can grate more than just cheeses? If you don't want to use a food processor, you can use a grater to grate up veggies. You can also grate vegan cheese for many recipes.

CONTAINERS

For this meal plan it will be useful for you to have 18 portion size containers available that are both freezer and microwave friendly. It should have a perfect tight lid. Glass containers are best as they are suitable for microwaving. They also don't have toxic chemicals leaching out of them either. A convenient storage container is a must for a healthy kitchen.

MASON JARS

These are great for keeping various ingredients in the freezer or cupboards. They can prevent freezer burns and keep its contents fresh. You should always leave some headspace in the jar when you freeze something. Use glass mason jars to help reduce the amount of plastic in the environment.

CHOPPING BOARD

You need to do a lot of cutting, and having a variety of chopping boards at hand can help prevent cross-contamination. Large bamboo chopping boards can last for a long time and are easier to maintain.

HOW TO DO A MEAL PREPARATION DAY? – ORGANIZATION TIPS

You want to choose 1 or 2 days during the week as your meal prep day(s). My favorite meal prep day is Sunday, but you are free to choose whichever day works best for you. The 1-day meal prep method can save you a lot of time. However, you need to make sure that you can store some of the meals in the freezer since not all the meals can last more than 4 days.

Here are some tips for the meal prep day:

- Have a maximum of three hours set aside for this task. This may seem a long time to spend in the kitchen but remember you are doing this meal prep to save time later in your week.
- Check beforehand if you are ready for meal prep or not. If you're meal prepping for an entire week on a Sunday, make sure you have all your ingredients and tools Saturday night.
- When you are buying your groceries, don't go on an empty stomach or without a list. Make a meal planned list of ingredients and stick to it.
- Store ingredients as soon as you come back from the store. Place it in the freezer if you are going to meal prep after a day

or two; otherwise, just put the cold ingredients in the fridge till the time comes.

- My suggestion is that you go through all the recipes for the week, and have all the ingredients that you need by your side. Next, read our meal prep day guide and follow the instructions. This way, you can stay organized and it will save you a lot of time.
- We have created a rough plan on the best way to create all your meals at once. This is the meal prep day guide, and it involves things like cooking all your different grains at the same time or preparing a sauce for your dinner while also preparing one of your breakfast items. It will seem like you are jumping between recipes but hopefully by the end of your 3 hours you will have all your recipes prepped and in containers ready for the week ahead.

MAKE MEAL PREPPING FUN

- Don't make this joyful experience into a tedious, labor-intensive job. Play your favorite music or listen to a podcast and get excited about how easy your week ahead will be.
- Take photos of your creations and share them on your social

media platforms to show your friends and family. You may just get some support and encouragement in return.

PANTRY STAPLES

Useful ingredients to have in your cupboards for the whole 28 days.

Spices:

- Salt
- Black pepper
- Cinnamon
- Smoked paprika
- Thyme
- Red Chilli powder
- Cumin
- Cloves
- Ginger
- Garlic
- Basil leaves

Oil:

- Coconut oil
- Olive oil
- Avocado oil

Sweeteners:

- Date sugar
- Pure maple syrup
- Coconut sugar
- Dates

Vinegar:

- Apple cider vinegar
- Balsamic vinegar
- Rice vinegar

Other ingredients:

- Nutritional Yeast
- Baking Powder

Portion Control:

If you want to succeed in the meal plan mentioned in this e-book, it's essential to keep an adequate portion size. The portion control in this meal prep guide is:

Breakfast:
between 250 – 350 calories per portion
Lunch:
between 350 – 400 calories per portion
Dinner:
between 350 – 400 degrees calories per portion
Plus snacks - make up 1200 to 1250 calories in a day

We have also provided modifications for extra calories if needed.

What to drink during this meal plan?

Water is going to be your primary source of hydration. Hydration is essential for this diet.

On average, women need to drink 2.2 liters of water while men need to drink about 3 liters.

Drinks to Avoid:

- Alcohol
- Sugary drinks (including sugar-free soft drinks)
- Tea and Coffee with sugar

Drinks to have:

- Water
- Sparkling Water
- Green Tea
- Herbal Teas

Tips for Consuming Enough Fluids

If you struggle with drinking water or are forgetful, you might want to try these tricks to help you stay hydrated.

- Carry a full water bottle with you all the time. This way you can quench your thirst on the go.
- Have a bottle or a glass of water by your bedside. You should drink before and after going to bed.
- If you are not enjoying the plain taste of water, try creating favored water using fresh herbs and fruits. Few of my favorite are rosemary & raspberry or mint & cucumber.

WEEK 1

WEEK 1 MEAL PREP GUIDE

Week 1 - Menu

Breakfast:
Breakfast Muesli
Tofu-Egg Salad Sandwich

Lunch & Dinner:
Millet and Lentil Salad
Herby Mushroom Patties
Tempeh Burger with Portobello Bun

Snacks:
Spinach and Avocado Smoothie
Raw Walnut Halves
Spiced Edamame Beans

WEEK 1 MEAL PLAN

YOUR HEALTHY MEAL PLAN

MONDAY

Breakfast: Breakfast Muesli
Snack: Spiced Edamame Beans
Lunch: Millet and Lentil Salad
Snack: Spinach and Avocado Smoothie
Dinner: Tempeh Burger with Portobello Bun

Calories: 1171.6
Carbohydrates: 99.5 g
Dietary Fiber: 44.5 g
Protein: 64.2 g
Fat: 61.6 g
Saturated Fat: 18.4 g
Net Carb: 54.9 g

TUESDAY

Breakfast: Tofu-Egg Salad Sandwich
Snack: Spinach and Avocado Smoothie
Lunch: Herby Mushroom Patties
Snack: Walnut
Dinner: Millet and Lentil Salad

Calories: 1227.2
Carbohydrates: 96.1 g
Dietary Fiber: 49.5 g
Protein: 64.9 g
Fat: 65.6 g
Saturated Fat: 12.3 g
Net Carb: 46.6 g

WEDNESDAY

Breakfast: Breakfast Muesli
Snack: Spiced Edamame Beans
Lunch: Millet and Lentil Salad
Snack: Walnut
Dinner: Tempeh Burger with Portobello Bun

Calories: 1133.6
Carbohydrates: 95.3 g
Dietary Fiber: 42.1 g
Protein: 61.3 g
Fat: 60.6 g
Saturated Fat: 15.6 g
Net Carb: 53.2 g

THURSDAY

Breakfast: Tofu-Egg Salad Sandwich
Snack: Spinach and Avocado Smoothie
Lunch: Herby Mushroom Patties
Snack: Spiced Edamame Beans
Dinner: Millet and Lentil Salad

Calories: 1198.2
Carbohydrates: 102.5 g
Dietary Fiber: 52.2 g
Protein: 69.8 g
Fat: 55.6 g
Saturated Fat: 11.7 g
Net Carb: 50.3 g

FRIDAY

Breakfast: Breakfast Muesli
Snack: Walnut
Lunch: Herby Mushroom Patties
Snack: Spinach and Avocado Smoothie
Dinner: Tempeh Burger with Portobello Bun

Calories: 1235.4
Carbohydrates: 80.4 g
Dietary Fiber: 34.6 g
Protein: 62.2 g
Fat: 76.8 g
Saturated Fat: 16.8 g
Net Carb: 45.7 g

SATURDAY

Breakfast: Tofu-Egg Salad Sandwich
Snack: Spiced Edamame Beans
Lunch: Tempeh Burger with Portobello Bun
Snack: Walnut
Dinner: Herby Mushroom Patties

Calories: 1202.7
Carbohydrates: 103.3g
Dietary Fiber: 52.1 g
Protein: 69.6 g
Fat: 58.4 g
Saturated Fat: 9.6 g
Net Carb: 51.3 g

2

WEEK 1 - SHOPPING LIST

WEEK 1 SHOPPING LIST

YOUR HEALTHY MEAL PREPARATION

Pantry Items
- [ ] 4 teaspoons flax oil
- [ ] 1/8 teaspoon liquid stevia
- [ ] ½ teaspoon ground Aleppo pepper
- [ ] 4 tablespoons hemp protein powder
- [ ] 4 tablespoons yeast flakes
- [ ] 4 ½ tablespoons of vanilla protein powder
- [ ] 3 tablespoons peanut butter powder
- [ ] ¼ teaspoon vanilla extract
- [ ] 1 tablespoon Dijon mustard
- [ ] 3 tablespoons chives
- [ ] ½ bunch of dill
- [ ] 1 cup vegan parmesan cheese

Vegetables
- [ ] 3 cups Brussels sprouts
- [ ] 1 ½ leek
- [ ] 3 green onions
- [ ] 3 cups sliced button mushrooms
- [ ] 1 small potato
- [ ] 8 Portobello mushrooms
- [ ] 2 large zucchinis
- [ ] 3 medium avocados
- [ ] 3 cups spinach leaves
- [ ] ½ cup vegetable stock

Protein
- [ ] 1 ¾ cups soy milk
- [ ] 4 ½ cups of coconut milk
- [ ] 18 ounces tofu, firm
- [ ] 16 ounces tempeh
- [ ] 1/3 cup mayonnaise, vegan

Beans, Legumes, Grains
- [ ] 2 ¼ cup millet
- [ ] 1 ½ cup brown lentils
- [ ] 2 cups edamame beans
- [ ] 6 slices of whole-wheat bread

Nuts, Seeds
- [ ] ¼ cup sunflower seeds
- [ ] ¼ cup pumpkin seeds
- [ ] ¼ cup coconut flakes
- [ ] 6 tablespoons hemp hearts
- [ ] 2 tablespoons pecans
- [ ] 4 tablespoons hemp seeds
- [ ] 20 whole walnuts

3

WEEK 1 - MEAL PREP DAY GUIDE

- Step 1: Go through all the recipes for week 1, and prepare all the ingredients that you need.
- Step 2: Prepare the muesli mixture for breakfast. Preheat the oven to 350 degrees F. Gather and prepare ingredients for muesli and then bake.
- Step 3: Gather the ingredients for the salad of the tofu-egg salad sandwich, prepare it, and then store it.
- Step 4: Cool the muesli and then store.
- Step 5: Marinate the tempeh for tempeh burger with Portobello bun recipe.
- Step 6: Bake sprouts and leeks for the lentil salad, and for this, set the oven for 425 and let it preheat. Meanwhile, cook the millet and lentils, and when done, let them cool completely.
- Step 7: When the oven has preheated, bake the sprouts and leeks.
- Step 8: Steam edamame beans and prepare the snack according to the instructions in the recipe for edamame beans with Aleppo pepper.
- Step 9: Prepare walnuts for snack and store.

- Step 10: Cook the mushrooms for mushroom patties and boil potatoes for it.
- Step 11: When sprouts, leeks, millet, and lentils have cooked and cooled, assemble the salad, and then store.
- Step 12: Prepare mushroom patties, fry, and then cool them and store.
- Step 13: Cook the marinated tempeh, broil mushroom caps, cool them, and then assemble burgers as per instructions in the recipe for tempeh burger with Portobello bun.
- Step 14: Prepare mason jars for smoothie and store.

When ready to eat:

Breakfast Muesli – add soy milk to muesli, heat in the microwave for 5 minutes.

Tofu-Egg Salad Sandwich – toast two bread slices, spread one portion of egg salad on it, and then cover with the other bread slice.

Millet and Lentil Salad – eat the salad as it is or bring the salad to room temperature and then enjoy.

Herby Mushroom Patties – reheat the patties in the microwave for 1 to 2 minutes until hot and then serve.

Tempeh Burger with Portobello Bun – reheat the burger in the microwave for 2 minutes until hot and then eat it.

Avocado and Spinach Smoothie – uncover a smoothie jar and pour in 1 ½ cup milk, puree by using an immersion blender until smooth and then serve.

Walnut – eat 5 walnuts about 2.5 ounces

Spiced Edamame Beans – ½ cup of edamame beans tossed with Aleppo pepper mixture

Modifications

1500 calories

- Day 1 – have 2 tempeh burgers with Portobello bun and zucchini fries for dinner
- Day 2 – have 7.5 ounces of walnuts as a snack
- Day 3 – have 2 tempeh burger with Portobello bun for dinner
- Day 4 – have 2 bowls of millet and lentil salad for dinner
- Day 5 – have 2 bowls of breakfast muesli for breakfast
- Day 6 – have 2 tofu-egg salad sandwich for breakfast

2000 calories

- Day 1 – have 2 bowls of muesli for breakfast and 1 1/2 cups edamame beans as a snack
- Day 2 – have 2 tofu-egg salad sandwiches for breakfast, 2 bowls of millet and lentil salad for dinner, and 2 glasses of avocado and spinach salad for a snack
- Day 3 – have 2 bowls of millet and lentil salad for lunch, have 2 tempeh burger with Portobello bun for dinner, 1 cup edamame beans, and 5 ounces of walnuts for a snack
- Day 4 – have 1 1/2 cup of edamame beans and 7.5 ounces walnuts for a snack
- Day 5 – have 2 bowls of breakfast muesli for breakfast, 1 1/2 tempeh burger with Portobello bun for dinner, 2 glasses of avocado and spinach smoothie 5 ounces of walnuts as a snack
- Day 6 – have two tofu-egg salad sandwiches for breakfast, 2 tempeh burger with Portobello bun for lunch, 5 ounces walnuts for a snack

WEEK 1 RECIPES

BREAKFAST MUESLI

Serves: 3
Total Time: 8 minutes
Prep Time: 10 minutes
Tags: low carb, high protein, sugar-free, dairy-free, egg-free

Ingredients:

For the Muesli:

- 3 tablespoons sunflower seeds
- 3 tablespoons pumpkin seeds
- 3 tablespoons coconut flakes, unsweetened
- 5 tablespoons hemp hearts
- 2 tablespoons pecans
- 1/8 teaspoon liquid stevia
- ¾ teaspoon ground cinnamon
- ¼ teaspoon vanilla extract, unsweetened

For Serving:

- 1 ½ cups / 375 ml soymilk, unsweetened

Directions:

1. Switch on the oven, then set it to 350 degrees F and let it preheat.
2. Take a large bowl, place all the ingredients for the muesli in it and then stir until well combined.
3. Spread the muesli mixture onto a rimmed baking pan and then bake for 8 minutes.
4. When done, let muesli cool completely, transfer into an airtight container, and let it rest at room temperature until required.
5. When ready to eat, transfer one-third of muesli in a heatproof bowl, pour in ½ cup milk, and stir until just mixed.
6. Microwave the muesli bowl for 5 minutes at high heat setting, stirring halfway, sprinkle with a pinch of cinnamon, and then serve.

Nutritional Values Per Serving

Calories: 277.7 kcal
Carbohydrates: 10.4 g
Dietary Fiber: 3.9 g
Protein: 11.1 g
Fat: 21.3 g
Saturated Fat: 5 g

2

TOFU-EGG SALAD SANDWICH

Serves: 3 sandwiches, 1 sandwich per serving
Total Time: 15 minutes
Prep Time: 10 minutes
Tags: low carb, high protein, dairy-free, egg-free, raw, sugar-free

Ingredients:

For the Salad:

- 14 ounces / 510 g tofu, firm, pressed, drained
- ¼ cup / 77 g vegan mayonnaise
- 1 tablespoon Dijon mustard
- ½ teaspoon turmeric powder
- ½ teaspoon salt
- 1/3 teaspoon ground black pepper
- 2 tablespoons chopped chives

For Serving:

- 6 slices of whole-wheat bread

Directions:

1. Place pressed and drained tofu on a cutting board and then cut it into cubes.
2. Prepare the dressing and for this, take a tall container, add all the ingredients in it for the salad except for tofu, celery, and chives and then mix by using a hand blender until creamy and smooth.
3. Add tofu cubes into the dressing, add celery and chives and then gently stir until combined.
4. Divide the salad evenly among three meal prep containers, shut with the lid, and then store in the refrigerator for up to 6 days.
5. When ready to eat, toast two bread slices, spread egg salad from one container, cover with the other bread slice, and then serve.

Nutritional Values Per Serving
Calories: 312 kcal

Carbohydrates: 31.1 g
Dietary Fiber: 21 g
Protein: 16.5 g
Fat: 13.8 g
Saturated Fat: 1.2 g

3

MILLET AND LENTIL SALAD

Serves: 4 bowls, 1 2-cups bowl per serving
Total Time: 1 hour and 15 minutes
Prep Time: 15 minutes
Tags: low carb, high protein, dairy-free, egg-free, gluten-free, nut-free, coconut-free, sugar-free

Ingredients:

- 2 ¼ cups / 210 g millet
- 3 cups / 465 g Brussels Sprouts, quartered
- 1 ½ cups / 288 g brown lentils, uncooked
- 1 ½ leek, ¼-inch sliced
- 3 green onions, green parts sliced only
- 1/3 teaspoon garlic powder
- 1 teaspoon salt
- 2 tablespoons olive oil
- 4 teaspoons flax oil
- 3 cups / 705 ml water, and more as needed

Directions:

1. Switch on the oven, then set it to 425 degrees F and let it preheat.
2. Meanwhile, cook the millet and for this, take a large pot half full with water, place it over medium-high heat and bring it to a boil.
3. Add millet into the boiling water, switch heat to medium level and then cook for 50 to 60 minutes, covering the pot with its lid.
4. In the meantime, cook the lentils and for this, place a medium pot over medium-high heat, pour in 3 cups of water, bring it to a boil, then add lentils, switch heat to medium level, and cook for 30 minutes until tender, covering the pot with its lid.
5. While millet and lentils cook, take a large casserole dish, place sprouts and leeks in it, drizzle with oil, sprinkle with ½ teaspoon salt and garlic powder, toss until coated, then cover the dish with foil and bake for 40 minutes.
6. When millet and lentils have cooked, drain them, transfer into a bowl, then add sprouts and let cool completely.

7. Then season with salt, add flax oil and green onions, toss until mixed and divide salad among four meal prep containers.

8. Cover the containers with its lid and then store it in the refrigerator for up to 6 days.

Nutritional Values Per Serving

Calories: 291.2 kcal

Carbohydrates: 34 g

Dietary Fiber: 15.3 g

Protein: 18.2 g

Fat: 9.8 g

Saturated Fat: 4.1 g

HERBY MUSHROOM PATTIES

Serves: 16 patties, 4 patties per serving
Total Time: 45 minutes
Prep Time: 15 minutes

Tags: low carb, high protein, dairy-free, egg-free, nut-free, soy-free, gluten-free, sugar-free

Ingredients:

For the Burger:

- 3 cups / 300 g sliced button mushrooms
- 1 small potato, skin on, boiled
- ½ bunch of dill, chopped
- 1 ¼ teaspoon salt
- 4 tablespoons hemp protein powder
- 2/3 teaspoon ground black pepper
- 2 teaspoons dried thyme
- 4 tablespoons yeast flakes, inactive
- 4 tablespoons hemp seeds
- 2 ½ tablespoons olive oil

Directions:

1. Take a large skillet pan, place it over medium heat, add 1 tablespoon oil, and when hot and add mushrooms.
2. Season onion with salt, black pepper, and thyme, stir until mixed and then cook for 10 minutes, cover the pan with its lid.
3. Meanwhile, peel the boiled potato, cut it into pieces, place them in a bowl, mash by using a fork and then stir in the yeast until combined.
4. Add cooked mushrooms mixture along with remaining ingredients and then stir by using a spoon until well combined.
5. Let the mixture cool until you can handle it with your hands and then shape the mixture into sixteen patties.
6. Take a large skillet pan, place it over medium-high heat, add

remaining oil and when hot, place prepared patties in it and then cook for 3 to 4 minutes per side until golden brown.

7. Let the patties cool completely, divide them evenly among four meal prep containers, shut with the lid, and then store in the refrigerator for up to 6 days.

Nutritional Values Per Serving

Calories: 326 kcal
Carbohydrates: 21.2 g
Dietary Fiber: 8 g
Protein: 21.2 g
Fat: 17 g
Saturated Fat: 1.8 g

5

TEMPEH BURGER WITH PORTOBELLO BUN AND ZUCCHINI FRIES

Serves: 4 burgers, 1 burger per serving
Total Time: 1 hour and 35 minutes
Prep Time: 1 hour and 15 minutes
Tags: low carb, high protein, egg-free, nut-free, gluten-free, sugar-free

Ingredients:

For the Burger:

- 8 ounces / 227.5 grams tempeh
- ½ teaspoon garlic powder
- ½ teaspoon onion powder
- ½ tablespoon dried thyme
- 1 tablespoons soy sauce
- 2 tablespoon olive oil, divided
- 1 tablespoon apple cider vinegar
- ¼ cup / 50 ml vegetable stock

For Zucchini Fries:

- 2 large zucchinis
- 1 cup grated vegan parmesan cheese
- 4 tablespoons dried oregano
- ¼ cup soy milk
- 1 teaspoon ground black pepper

For Serving:

- 4 whole Portobello mushrooms
- 2 teaspoons salt
- 1 teaspoon ground black pepper
- 1 tablespoon olive oil
- 4 leaves of lettuce
- 4 slices of tomato

Directions:

1. Prepare the tempeh and for this, cut it into ½-inch slices and then place them in a shallow dish.
2. Take a medium bowl, place remaining ingredients for the burger in it except for oil, whisk until combined, and then pour over tempeh pieces.
3. Toss until well coated and then marinate the tempeh slices for a minimum of 1 hour in the refrigerator.
4. Meanwhile, prepare the zucchini fries, and for this, switch on the oven, set it to 425 degrees F, and then cut zucchini into sticks.
5. Place cheese in a shallow dish, add black pepper and oregano, and then stir until mixed.
6. Take a separate shallow dish, and then pour in the milk.
7. Take a large baking sheet and then line it with a parchment sheet.
8. Working on one zucchini stick at a time, dip it into the milk, coat in cheese mixture, and then place on the prepared baking sheet.
9. Repeat with the remaining zucchini chips and then bake them for 25 minutes until golden brown, turning halfway.
10. Then take a large frying pan, place it over medium-high heat, add oil and when hot, place marinated tempeh slices in it, and then cook for 3 to 4 minutes per side until golden and crisp.
11. Pour the marinade over slices of tempeh, switch heat to medium level and then continue cooking for 15 minutes until tempeh has mostly absorbed all its sauce.
12. In the meantime, prepare the mushrooms and for this, remove the stem from each mushroom, clean, rinse and pat dry them, brush each mushroom with ¼ tablespoon oil and then season with ½ teaspoon salt and ¼ teaspoon black pepper.
13. Switch on the broiler and when it preheats, place mushroom caps under it and then cook for 5 minutes per side until tender, set aside until required.
14. When tempeh has cooked, assemble the burger and for this, a

mushroom cap in a meal prep container, and top with tempeh slices.

15. Cover tempeh with a tomato slice and a lettuce leaf and then add one-fourth portion of zucchini fries.

16. Prepare remaining burgers in the same manner, shut each container with its lid and then store in the refrigerator for up to 6 days.

Nutritional Values Per Serving

Calories: 333.6 kcal
Carbohydrates: 38.9 g
Dietary Fiber: 17.5 g
Protein: 20.1 g
Fat: 13.5 g
Saturated Fat: 4.7 g

6

AVOCADO AND SPINACH SMOOTHIE

Serves: 3 glasses, 1 glass per serving
Total Time: 5 minutes
Prep Time: 5 minutes

Tags: low carb, high protein, nut-free, soy-free, gluten-free, sugar-free

Ingredients:

- 3 medium avocado, peeled, pitted, flesh diced
- 3 scoops of vanilla protein powder, sugar-free
- 3 cups / 90 grams baby spinach, fresh
- 3 tablespoons peanut butter powder
- 4 ½ cups / 1125 ml coconut milk, unsweetened

Directions:

1. Take a mason jar, place pieces of 1 avocado in it, add 1 cup spinach leaves and then add vanilla protein powder and peanut butter powder.
2. Shut the jar with its lid and then prepare two more jars in the same manner.
3. Store the jars in the refrigerator for up to 6 days and when ready to drink, uncover a jar and pour in 1 ½ cup milk and then puree by using an immersion blender until smooth.

Nutritional Values Per Serving

Calories: 168 kcal

Carbohydrates: 7 g

Dietary Fiber: 3.8 g

Protein: 6 g

Fat: 14 g

Saturated Fat: 4 g

7

SPICED EDAMAME BEANS

Serves: 2 cups, ½ cup per serving
Total Time: 5 minutes
Prep Time: 5 minutes

Tags: low carb, high protein, dairy-free, egg-free, nut-free, soy-free, gluten-free, sugar-free

Ingredients:

- 2 cups / 310 g edamame beans, in pods
- ½ teaspoon ground Aleppo pepper
- 3 tablespoons water

Directions:

1. Place beans in a heatproof bowl, drizzle with water, cover the bowl with a plastic wrap, and then microwave for 2 to 3 minutes until steamed.
2. Drain the beans, pat dry with paper towels and then sprinkle with pepper.
3. Divide spiced beans evenly among four mini meal prep containers or plastic bags and seal them.

Nutritional Values Per Serving

Calories: 101 kcal
Carbohydrates: 9.2 g
Dietary Fiber: 4.1 g
Protein: 8 g
Fat: 3 g
Saturated Fat: 0.6 g

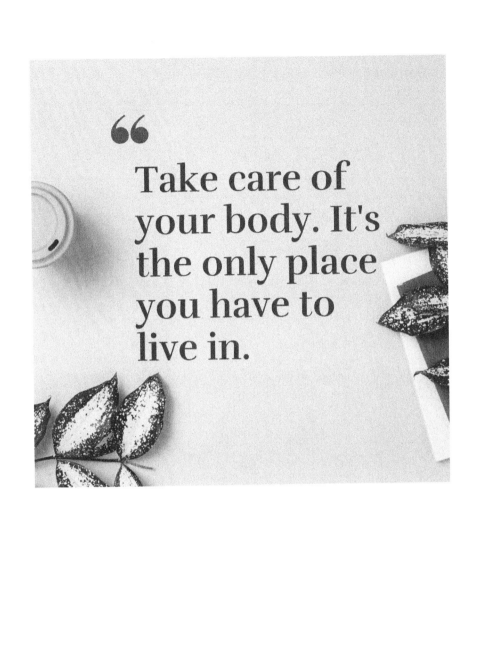

" Take care of your body. It's the only place you have to live in.

WEEK 2

WEEK 2 MEAL PREP GUIDE

Week 2 - Menu

Breakfast:
Tofu Scramble
Chocolate Chia Pudding

Lunch & Dinner:
Sesame Salad with Baked Tofu
Peanut Butter Tempeh and Rice
Spaghetti Squash with Peanut Sauce

Snacks:
Carrot Cake Smoothie
Pistachios
Banana and Peanut Butter

WEEK 2 MEAL PLAN

YOUR HEALTHY MEAL PLAN

MONDAY

Breakfast: Tofu Scramble
Snack: Banana and Peanut Butter Snack
Lunch: Sesame Salad with Baked Tofu
Snack: Carrot Cake Smoothie
Dinner: Spaghetti Squash Noodles with Peanut Sauce

Calories: 1252
Carbohydrates: 88.9 g
Dietary Fiber: 49.8 g
Protein: 80.5 g
Fat: 50.1 g
Saturated Fat: 7.8 g
Net Carb: 39.1 g

TUESDAY

Breakfast: Chocolate Chia Pudding
Snack: Carrot Cake Smoothie
Lunch: Peanut Butter Tempeh and Rice Bowl
Snack: Pistachios
Dinner: Sesame Salad with Baked Tofu

Calories: 1194.8
Carbohydrates: 104.2 g
Dietary Fiber: 59.3 g
Protein: 64.8 g
Fat: 62.8 g
Saturated Fat: 11.1 g
Net Carb: 44.8 g

WEDNESDAY

Breakfast: Tofu Scramble
Snack: Banana and Peanut Butter Snack
Lunch: Sesame Salad with Baked Tofu
Snack: Pistachios
Dinner: Spaghetti Squash Noodles with Peanut Sauce

Calories: 1244
Carbohydrates: 78.4 g
Dietary Fiber: 42.1 g
Protein: 74.7 g
Fat: 56.3 g
Saturated Fat: 7.7 g
Net Carb: 36.3 g

THURSDAY

Breakfast: Chocolate Chia Pudding
Snack: Carrot Cake Smoothie
Lunch: Peanut Butter Tempeh and Rice
Snack: Banana and Peanut Butter Snack
Dinner: Sesame Salad with Baked Tofu

Calories: 1216.8
Carbohydrates: 114.8 g
Dietary Fiber: 64.7 g
Protein: 68.7 g
Fat: 57.9 g
Saturated Fat: 10.7 g
Net Carb: 50.1 g

FRIDAY

Breakfast: Tofu Scramble
Snack: Pistachios
Lunch: Peanut Butter Tempeh and Rice Bowl
Snack: Carrot Cake Smoothie
Dinner: Spaghetti Squash Noodles with
Peanut Sauce

Calories: 1198.7
Carbohydrates: 83.04 g
Dietary Fiber: 45.5 g
Protein: 81 g
Fat: 46.3 g
Saturated Fat: 10.6 g
Net Carb: 37.4 g

SATURDAY

Breakfast: Chocolate Chia Pudding
Snack: Banana and Peanut Butter Snack
Lunch: Spaghetti Squash Noodles with
Peanut Sauce
Snack: Pistachios
Dinner: Peanut Butter Tempeh and Rice Bowl

Calories: 1208.4
Carbohydrates: 107.2 g
Dietary Fiber: 58.3 g
Protein: 59.9 g
Fat: 62.64 g
Saturated Fat: 11.4 g
Net Carb: 48.8 g

2

WEEK 2 - SHOPPING LIST

WEEK 2 SHOPPING LIST

YOUR HEALTHY MEAL PREPARATION

Pantry Items

- ☐ 4 ½ tablespoons almond butter
- ☐ ¾ cup and ½ tablespoon peanut butter
- ☐ 9 tablespoons nutritional yeast
- ☐ 1 tablespoon coconut flakes
- ☐ 1 ¼ scoop of vanilla protein powder
- ☐ 4 ½ tablespoons Dijon mustard
- ☐ ½ cup of soy sauce
- ☐ 2 tablespoons red chili sauce
- ☐ 7 tablespoons maple syrup
- ☐ 4 tablespoons coconut sugar
- ☐ 2 teaspoons agave syrup
- ☐ 6 tablespoons cocoa powder
- ☐ 1 ½ tablespoon sesame oil
- ☐ 4 tablespoons apple cider vinegar
- ☐ 2 tablespoons hoisin sauce

Vegetables

- ☐ 2 tablespoons grated ginger
- ☐ 3 teaspoons minced garlic
- ☐ 12 cups mixed greens
- ☐ 5 ounces purple cabbage
- ☐ 1 1/3 cup cauliflower florets
- ☐ 2 limes
- ☐ 2 cups carrot matchsticks
- ☐ 3 medium carrot
- ☐ 2 cups sliced snap peas

- ☐ 3 scallion
- ☐ 2 green onions
- ☐ ¼ cup pitted kalamata olives
- ☐ ¼ cup cherry tomatoes
- ☐ 2 pounds spaghetti squash
- ☐ 1 cup shelled edamame beans
- ☐ ¼ cup cilantro
- ☐ ½ medium red bell pepper
- ☐ ½ cup pineapple pieces
- ☐ 1 frozen banana
- ☐ 2 large bananas, fresh

Protein

- ☐ 44.6 ounces tofu, extra-firm
- ☐ 22 ounces tempeh
- ☐ 1 1/3 cup soy milk
- ☐ 3 ½ cups almond milk

Beans, Legumes, Grains

- ☐ 6.5 ounces brown rice

Nuts, Seeds

- ☐ ¼ cup peanuts
- ☐ ¾ cup chia seeds
- ☐ 6 tablespoons hemp seeds
- ☐ 1 tablespoon sesame seeds
- ☐ 1 tablespoon flaxseed
- ☐ 6 ounces pistachios

WEEK 2 - MEAL PREP DAY GUIDE

- Step 1: Go through all the recipes for week 2, and prepare all the ingredients that you need.
- Step 2: Prepare the sauce for the peanut butter tempeh and rice bowl, add tempeh, and let them marinate for 3 hours.
- Step 3: Prepare the chocolate chia breakfast pudding and let it rest for 45 minutes until thickened.
- Step 4: Prepare the sesame salad with baked tofu and for this, preheat the oven to 400 degrees F.
- Step 5: Gather the ingredients for the tofu scramble, prepare it, cool it completely, and then store it.
- Step 6: Prepare tofu for the sesame salad with baked tofu and bake it. Prepare the squash for the spaghetti noodles with peanut sauce and bake it.
- Step 7: Gather the ingredients for the sesame salad with baked tofu salad dressing and prepare it.
- Step 8: Cook the brown rice for the peanut butter tempeh and rice bowl and let it cool completely.
- Step 9: Cool the baked tofu completely.
- Step 10: Cool the baked squash completely, assemble spaghetti

squash noodles with peanut sauce according to its recipe and then store it.

- Step 11: Prepare the cabbage for the peanut butter tempeh and rice bowl and set it aside until required.
- Step 12: Prepare the sauce for the spaghetti noodles with peanut sauce and set it aside until required.
- Step 13: Bake the tempeh for the peanut butter tempeh and rice bowl, and for this, preheat the oven to 375 degrees F.
- Step 14: Assemble the sesame salad with baked tofu and then store.
- Step 15: Bake the tempeh and then cool it completely.
- Step 16: Prepare mason jars for smoothie and store.
- Step 17: Prepare the banana and peanut butter snacks and store them.
- Step 18: Prepare pistachios for a snack and store them.
- Step 19: Assemble the peanut butter tempeh and rice bowl as per instructions in its recipe and then store it.

When ready to eat:

Tofu Scramble – reheat the tofu scramble in the microwave for 1 to 2 minutes until hot and then serve.

Chocolate Chia Pudding – let the pudding rest at room temperature for 15 minutes and then serve.

Sesame Salad with Baked Tofu – eat the salad as it is or bring the salad to room temperature and then enjoy it.

Peanut Butter Tempeh and Rice Bowl – reheat the bowl for 1 to 2 minutes until hot and then serve.

Spaghetti Squash Noodles with Peanut Sauce – reheat the noodles for 1 to 2 minutes until hot, toss until just mixed, and then serve.

Carrot Cake Smoothie – uncover a smoothie jar and pour in ½ cup milk, puree by using an immersion blender until smooth, and then serve.

Pistachios – eat 1.5 ounces pistachios as a snack

Banana and Peanut Butter Snack – eat it as it is

Modifications

1500 calories

- Day 1 – have 2 glasses of carrot cake smoothie and 2 banana and peanut butter snacks
- Day 2 – have 2 servings of peanut butter tempeh and rice
- Day 3 – have 2 servings of tofu scramble
- Day 4 – have 2 servings of chocolate chia pudding
- Day 5 – have 2 servings of peanut butter tempeh and rice
- Day 6 – have 2 servings of chocolate chia pudding

2000 calories

- Day 1 – have 2 servings of tofu scramble for breakfast, 2 servings of sesame salad with baked tofu for lunch, and 2 glasses of carrot cake smoothie as a snack
- Day 2 – have 2 servings of chocolate chia pudding for breakfast, 2 servings of peanut butter tempeh and rice for lunch, 2 glasses of carrot cake smoothie, and 3 ounces of pistachios as a snack
- Day 3 – have 2 servings of tofu scramble for breakfast, 2 servings of sesame salad with baked tofu for lunch, and 3 ounces of pistachios as a snack
- Day 4 – have 2 servings of peanut butter tempeh and rice for lunch, 2 servings of sesame salad with baked tofu for dinner, and 2 glasses of carrot cake smoothie as a snack
- Day 5 – have 2 servings of peanut butter tempeh and rice for lunch, 2 servings of spaghetti squash with peanut sauce for dinner, and 2 glasses of carrot cake smoothie as a snack
- Day 6 – have 2 servings of spaghetti squash with peanut sauce for lunch, 2 servings of peanut butter tempeh rice for dinner, and 3 ounces of pistachios as a snack

WEEK 2 RECIPES

TOFU SCRAMBLE

Serves: 3 plates, 1 plate per serving
Total Time: 15 minutes
Prep Time: 5 minutes

Tags: low carb, high protein, sugar-free, dairy-free, egg-free, gluten-free, coconut-free

Ingredients:

- 18 ounces tofu, extra-firm, pressed, drained
- 9 tablespoons nutritional yeast
- 2 ¼ teaspoon garlic powder
- 2 ¼ teaspoon onion powder
- 2 ¼ teaspoons ground turmeric
- 2 ¼ teaspoons paprika
- 2 ¼ teaspoons sea salt
- 1 ½ teaspoon ground black pepper
- 4 ½ teaspoons Dijon mustard
- 4 ½ tablespoons almond butter
- 1 1/3 cup soy milk

Directions:

1. Place tofu in a large bowl, and mash it.
2. Place onion powder in a separate bowl, add garlic powder, salt, paprika, turmeric, yeast, and mustard, stir until combined, and then whisk in milk until well combined.
3. Place a large frying pan over medium-high heat, add butter and when hot, add mashed tofu and then cook for 10 to 12 minutes until golden brown.
4. Then pour in the sauce, stir until just mixed and continue cooking for 3 to 5 minutes until the tofu has absorbed the sauce.
5. When done, remove the pan from heat, distribute tofu evenly among three meal prep containers, and let it cool at room temperature.

6. Then cover the containers with its lid and store in the refrigerator for up to 6 days.

Nutritional Values Per Serving

Calories: 301 kcal
Carbohydrates: 5.7 g
Dietary Fiber: 2.25 g
Protein: 30.4 g
Fat: 1.4 g
Saturated Fat: 0.5 g

2

CHOCOLATE CHIA BREAKFAST PUDDING

Serves: 3 bowls, 1 bowl per serving
Total Time: 50 minutes
Prep Time: 5 minutes

Tags: low carb, high protein, dairy-free, egg-free, raw, sugar-free, gluten-free, coconut-free

Ingredients:

- ¾ cup chia seeds
- 6 tablespoons maple syrup
- 6 tablespoons hemp seeds
- 6 tablespoons cocoa powder, unsweetened
- 1 ½ cup water
- 1 ½ cup almond milk, unsweetened

Directions:

1. Take a large bowl, place all the ingredients in it and then stir until combined and well incorporated.
2. Place the pudding bowl into the refrigerator and then let it rest for 45 minutes until thickened.
3. Then divide the pudding evenly among three mason jars, cover with the lid and then refrigerate it for 6 days.

Nutritional Values Per Serving

Calories: 297 kcal
Carbohydrates: 29.8 g
Dietary Fiber: 17.4 g
Protein: 11.2 g
Fat: 16.3 g
Saturated Fat: 1.7 g

SESAME SALAD WITH BAKED TOFU

Serves: 4 bowls, 1 bowl per serving
Total Time: 30 minutes
Prep Time: 10 minutes

Tags: low carb, high protein, dairy-free, egg-free, gluten-free, nut-free, coconut-free, sugar-free

Ingredients:

- 12 cups mixed greens
- 3 cups cubed tofu, about 12-ounces
- 2 cups carrot matchsticks
- 2 cups sliced snap peas
- 1 tablespoon olive oil

For the Dressing:

- 1 scallion, minced
- 1 tablespoon toasted sesame seeds
- 1 tablespoon toasted sesame oil
- 3 tablespoons apple cider vinegar
- 2 tablespoons hoisin sauce
- 3 tablespoons olive oil

Directions:

1. Switch on the oven, then set it to 400 degrees F and let it preheat.
2. Meanwhile, spread tofu cubes on a baking sheet, drizzle with oil and then toss until coated.
3. Bake the tofu pieces for 20 minutes until crisp, turning halfway through and then set aside until required.
4. Meanwhile, prepare the salad dressing and for this, place all of its ingredients in a small bowl and then stir until combined.
5. Divide the salad dressing evenly between four mason jars and then add 3 cups of mixed greens into each Mason jar.

6. Top greens in each jar with ¾ cup of tofu, ½ cup carrot matchsticks, and ½ cup snap peas.

7. Cover the Mason jar with its lid and then refrigerate the salad for up to 6 days.

Nutritional Values Per Serving

Calories: 335.5 kcal
Carbohydrates: 23.3 g
Dietary Fiber: 14.4 g
Protein: 17.1 g
Fat: 20.7 g
Saturated Fat: 2.2 g

4

PEANUT BUTTER TEMPEH AND RICE BOWL

Serves: 4 bowls, 1 bowl per serving
Total Time: 45 minutes
Prep Time: 15 minutes

Tags: low carb, high protein, dairy-free, egg-free, nut-free, soy-free, gluten-free, sugar-free

Ingredients:

- 22 ounces tempeh
- 6.5 ounces brown rice, uncooked
- 2 green onions, chopped
- Coconut oil for greasing

For the Sauce:

- 4 tablespoons peanut butter
- 4 tablespoons soy sauce
- 4 tablespoons coconut sugar
- 2 tablespoons red chili sauce
- 2 teaspoons apple cider vinegar
- 2 tablespoons grated ginger
- 2 teaspoons minced garlic
- 6 tablespoon water

For the Cabbage:

- 5-ounce purple cabbage, shredded
- 1 lime, juiced
- 2 teaspoons agave syrup
- 3 teaspoons sesame oil

Directions:

1. Prepare the sauce and for this, place all of its ingredients in a large bowl and then whisk until combined.

2. Then prepare tempeh and for this, cut it into 1-inch cubes.

3. Transfer tempeh pieces into the bowl containing the sauce, stir until coated, cover the bowl with its lid and then let it marinate for a minimum of 3 hours.

4. Meanwhile, cook the brown rice according to the instructions on its package and set aside until required.

5. When ready to bake, switch on the oven, then set it to 375 degrees F and let it preheat.

6. Take a non-stick baking sheet, grease it with coconut oil, spread tempeh pieces on it in a single layer, reserve the marinade, and then bake for 25 to 30 minutes until cooked, turning halfway.

7. While tempeh is baked, prepare the cabbage, and for this, place all of its ingredients in a large bowl, stir until combined, and let it marinate until required.

8. When tempeh has baked, let it cool completely and, in the meantime, distribute rice evenly among four meal prep containers.

9. Top the rice with cooled tempeh and cabbage mixture, sprinkle with green onions, drizzle with reserved marinade, cover the containers with its lid and then store it in the refrigerator for up to 6 days.

Nutritional Values Per Serving

Calories: 304 kcal
Carbohydrates: 28 g
Dietary Fiber: 15.5 g
Protein: 21.5 g
Fat: 12 g
Saturated Fat: 4.7 g

5

SPAGHETTI SQUASH NOODLES WITH PEANUT SAUCE

Serves: 4 cups, 1 cup per serving
Total Time: 1 hour
Prep Time: 15 minutes
Tags: low carb, high protein, dairy-free, egg-free, gluten-free, sugar-free, coconut-free

Ingredients:

- 2 pounds spaghetti squash
- 1 cup shelled edamame beans, frozen
- 1 medium carrot, shredded
- ½ cup sliced red bell pepper
- ¼ cup sliced scallion
- ¼ cup chopped cilantro
- ¼ cup cherry tomatoes, cut in half
- ¼ cup pitted kalamata olives
- ¼ cup chopped roasted peanut, unsalted
- 4 wedges of lime

For the Sauce:

- 1 teaspoon minced garlic
- ½ teaspoon red pepper flakes
- 1 tablespoon maple syrup
- ½ cup peanut butter
- 1 tablespoon apple cider vinegar
- ¼ cup of soy sauce
- ¼ cup of water

Directions:

1. Switch on the oven, then set it to 400 degrees F and let it preheat.
2. Meanwhile, cut the squash in half, and then arrange them cut-side down on a rimmed baking sheet.
3. Bake the squash pieces for 40 to 50 minutes until tender, and when done, let the squash cool for 10 minutes.
4. Then scrape the flesh of squash by running a fork lengthwise, transfer the squash noodles to a large bowl and cool it completely.
5. While squash bakes, prepare the sauce and for this, place all of

its ingredients in a bowl, whisk until smooth, and then distribute the sauce evenly among four meal prep containers.

6. Add cooled squash along with carrot, edamame, bell pepper, cherry tomatoes, olives and scallion, sprinkle cilantro and peanuts on top, add a lime wedge, then cover the containers with its lid and then store it in the refrigerator for up to 6 days.

Nutritional Values Per Serving

Calories: 335.4 kcal
Carbohydrates: 26.4 g
Dietary Fiber: 15.8 g
Protein: 14.1 g
Fat: 19.2 g
Saturated Fat: 2.9 g

6

CARROT CAKE SMOOTHIE

Serves: 4 glasses, 1 glass per serving
Total Time: 5 minutes
Prep Time: 5 minutes
Tags: low carb, high protein, nut-free, soy-free, gluten-free, sugar-free

Ingredients:

- 1 cup diced carrot
- 1 1/3 cup frozen cauliflower florets
- ½ cup pineapple pieces
- 1 of a frozen banana
- 1 tablespoon flaxseed
- 1 tablespoon coconut flakes
- 1 teaspoon ground cinnamon
- 1 scoop of vanilla protein powder
- 2 cups almond milk, unsweetened

Directions:

1. Take three Mason jar and then add ¼ cup carrot, 1/3 cup cauliflower florets, 2 tablespoons pineapple, and ¼ of banana in it.
2. Top with ¼ tablespoon flaxseed, ¼ tablespoon coconut flakes, ¼ scoop of protein powder, and ¼ teaspoon cinnamon, and then shut the jars with its lid.
3. Store the jars in the refrigerator for up to 6 days and when ready to drink, uncover a jar and pour in ½ cup milk and then puree by using an immersion blender until smooth.

Nutritional Values Per Serving

Calories: 133.3 kcal
Carbohydrates: 16.8 g
Dietary Fiber: 9.9 g
Protein: 10.4 g
Fat: 3.8 g
Saturated Fat: 1.3 g

7

BANANA AND PEANUT BUTTER SNACK

Serves: 4 snacks, 1 snack per serving
Total Time: 5 minutes
Prep Time: 5 minutes
Tags: low carb, high protein, soy-free, gluten-free, sugar-free

Ingredients:

- 2 large bananas
- ¼ scoop vanilla protein powder
- 1 ½ tablespoons peanut butter
- ½ tablespoon water

Directions:

1. Place peanut butter in a small bowl, add protein powder and water and then stir until a soft dough comes together.
2. Cut each banana in two pieces, slice each piece of banana lengthwise, smear nut mixture on top of four banana slices, and then cover with the other half.
3. Wrap banana tightly with a plastic wrap, make sure to remove as much as possible, and then store in the refrigerator for up to 6 days.

Nutritional Values Per Serving

Calories: 147 kcal
Carbohydrates: 16.9 g
Dietary Fiber: 7.5 g
Protein: 8.5 g
Fat: 5.1 g
Saturated Fat: 0.9 g

66

EAT LOTS OF
FRESH
VEGETABLES
, DRINK
WATER,
EXERCISE
OFTEN, AND
MEDITATE
DAILY.

Gretchen Bleiler

WEEK 3

WEEK 3 MEAL PREP GUIDE

Week 3 - Menu

Breakfast:
Pancakes with Berries
Breakfast Oats and Quinoa with Fruits

Lunch & Dinner:
White Bean Sandwich with Kale
Vegetable Burger with Broccoli and Squash
Black Bean-Quinoa Buddha Bowl

Snacks:
Chocolate Protein Shake
Pumpkin Seeds
Air-popped Popcorns

WEEK 3 MEAL PLAN

YOUR HEALTHY MEAL PLAN

MONDAY

Breakfast: Pancakes with Berries
Snack: Air-popped Popcorns
Lunch: White Bean Sandwich with Kale
Snack: Chocolate Protein Shake
Dinner: Black Bean-Quinoa Buddha Bowl

Calories: 1201
Carbohydrates: 132.4
Dietary Fiber: 85
Protein: 64.8
Fat: 44.4
Saturated Fat: 11.1
Net Carb: 47.4

TUESDAY

Breakfast: Breakfast Oats & Quinoa with Fruits
Snack: Chocolate Protein Shake
Lunch: Vegetable Burger with Broccoli and Squash
Snack: Pumpkin Seeds
Dinner: White Bean Sandwich with Kale

Calories: 1097.2
Carbohydrates: 150.5
Dietary Fiber: 96.1
Protein: 61.8
Fat: 26.8
Saturated Fat: 26.8
Net Carb: 4.5

WEDNESDAY

Breakfast: Pancakes with Berries
Snack: Air-popped Popcorns
Lunch: White Bean Sandwich with Kale
Snack: Pumpkin Seeds
Dinner: Black Bean-Quinoa Buddha Bowl

Calories: 1120.6
Carbohydrates: 136
Dietary Fiber: 86.7
Protein: 52.07
Fat: 39.5
Saturated Fat: 10.3
Net Carb: 49.3

THURSDAY

Breakfast: Breakfast Oats & Quinoa with Fruits
Snack: Chocolate Protein Shake
Lunch: Vegetable Burger with Broccoli and Squash
Snack: Air-popped Popcorns
Dinner: White Bean Sandwich with Kale

Calories: 1196.2
Carbohydrates: 142.3
Dietary Fiber: 91.8
Protein: 67.3
Fat: 38.6
Saturated Fat: 6.9
Net Carb: 50.5

FRIDAY

Breakfast: Pancakes with Berries
Snack: Pumpkin Seeds
Lunch: Vegetable Burger with Broccoli and Squash
Snack: Chocolate Protein Shake
Dinner: Black Bean-Quinoa Buddha Bowl

Calories: 1081.2
Carbohydrates: 145.5
Dietary Fiber: 95.1
Protein: 56.7
Fat: 29.3
Saturated Fat: 7.8
Net Carb: 50.4

SATURDAY

Breakfast: Breakfast Oats and Quinoa with Fruits
Snack: Air-popped Popcorns
Lunch: Black Bean-Quinoa Buddha Bowl
Snack: Pumpkin Seeds
Dinner: Vegetable Burger with Broccoli and Squash

Calories: 1103
Carbohydrates: 145.3
Dietary Fiber: 95.6
Protein: 55.2
Fat: 32.3
Saturated Fat: 6.1
Net Carb: 49.7

2

WEEK 3 - SHOPPING LIST

WEEK 3 SHOPPING LIST

YOUR HEALTHY MEAL PREPARATION

Pantry Items

- [ ] 2 teaspoons baking powder
- [ ] 3 teaspoons honey
- [ ] 3 teaspoons ground cinnamon
- [ ] ¼ teaspoon ground cumin
- [ ] 1 teaspoon vanilla extract
- [ ] 2 tablespoons coconut oil
- [ ] 4 tablespoons MCT oil

Vegetables and Fruits

- [ ] 2 cups blackberries
- [ ] ¾ cup diced peaches, fresh
- [ ] ¾ of a large banana, peeled, mashed
- [ ] ¾ cup blueberries, fresh
- [ ] ¾ cup raspberries, fresh
- [ ] 2 large bunches of kale
- [ ] ¼ of a medium white onion
- [ ] 4 medium tomatoes
- [ ] 1 medium jalapeno pepper
- [ ] 4 cups sliced cucumber
- [ ] 2 cups broccoli florets
- [ ] 8 ounces frozen mixed vegetables
- [ ] 3 cups cubes of squash
- [ ] 1 avocado
- [ ] ¼ cup chopped cilantro
- [ ] ¼ cup minced cilantro

Protein

- [ ] 6 tablespoons vanilla protein powder
- [ ] 1 ¼ cups chocolate-flavored protein powder
- [ ] 7 ¾ cups almond milk

Beans, Legumes, Grains

- [ ] 1 ½ cup white whole-wheat flour
- [ ] ¾ cup rolled oats
- [ ] 3 tablespoons flaxseed
- [ ] 2 ¼ cups quinoa
- [ ] 3 cups canned black beans
- [ ] 8 ounce canned white beans
- [ ] 2 cups canned chickpeas
- [ ] 4 tablespoons chickpea flour
- [ ] 8 slices of whole-wheat bread
- [ ] 4 whole-wheat burger bun

Nuts, Seeds

- [ ] 4 tablespoons peanut butter
- [ ] 3 teaspoons flax seed
- [ ] 8 tablespoons peanut powder

WEEK 3 - MEAL PREP DAY GUIDE

- Step 1: Go through all the recipes for week 3, and prepare all the ingredients that you need.
- Step 2: Set the temperature to 400 degrees F and let it preheat.
- Step 3: Prepare the kale for the white bean sandwich with kale, and then prepare the broccoli florets and squash pieces for the vegetable burger with broccoli and squash.
- Step 4: Arrange the baking sheets of kale, broccoli florets, and squash pieces into the preheated oven and let the vegetables accordingly.
- Step 5: Cook the quinoa for breakfast oats and quinoa with fruits and black bean-quinoa Buddha bowl and let it cool completely.
- Step 6: When the kale has baked, let it cool completely.
- Step 7: While quinoa cooks, prepare the batter for pancakes and let it rest for 15 minutes.
- Step 8: Cook the pancakes, let them cool completely, and then store them with berries and peanut butter.
- Step 9: Assemble the breakfast oats and quinoa with fruits and then store the containers.

- Step 10: Gather the ingredients for white beans for white bean sandwich with kale, assemble the sandwiches, and store them.
- Step 11: Gather the ingredients for the chickpea patties in the vegetable burger with broccoli and squash, prepare and fry them and then let them cool completely.
- Step 12: Assemble the black bean-quinoa Buddha bowl and then store its meal prep containers with avocado
- Step 13: Prepare the hummus and pico de gallo and then store these dip in meal prep containers.
- Step 14: Prepare mason jars for smoothie and store.
- Step 15: Prepare the banana and peanut butter snacks and store them.
- Step 16: Store ¼ cup of pumpkin seeds per serving in meal prep bags and store them.
- Step 17: Prepare the popcorn by following the instructions on its packages and then store them.
- Step 18: Assemble the vegetable burgers and then store them with roasted broccoli florets and squash.

When ready to eat:

Pancakes with Berries – reheat the pancakes in the microwave for 1 to 2 minutes until hot, drizzle with peanut butter and then serve with blackberries.

Breakfast Oats and Quinoa with Fruits – let the oats rest at room temperature for 15 minutes and then serve.

White Bean Sandwich with Kale – bring the sandwich at room temperature or enjoy it straight away.

Vegetable Burger with Broccoli and Squash – reheat the burgers, broccoli florets, and squash in the microwave for 1 to 2 minutes until hot, drizzle with peanut butter and then serve.

Black Bean-Quinoa Buddha Bowl – reheat the black bean and quinoa bowl in the microwave for 1 to 2 minutes until hot, assemble the bowl as per the last step in the recipe and then serve.

Chocolate Protein Shake – uncover a smoothie jar and pour in ½ cup ice cubes, puree by using an immersion blender until smooth, and then serve.

Pumpkin Seeds – eat ¼ cup of pumpkin seeds as a snack.

Air-popped Popcorns – eat 2 cups of popcorns as a snack.

Modifications

1500 calories

- Day 1 – have 2 servings of pancake for breakfast, and 2 glasses of chocolate protein shake as a snack
- Day 2 – have 2 servings of breakfast oats and quinoa with fruits for breakfast and 1/2 cup more chocolate protein shake as a snack
- Day 3 – have 2 servings of pancakes with berries for breakfast and 2 servings of pumpkin seeds as a snack
- Day 4 – have 2 servings of white bean sandwich with kale for dinner and 4 cups air-popped popcorns as a snack
- Day 5 – have 2 servings of vegetable burger with broccoli and squash for lunch
- Day 6 – have 2 servings of breakfast oats and quinoa with fruits for breakfast and 4 cups of air-popped popcorns as a snack

2000 calories

- Day 1 – have 2 servings of white bean sandwich with kale for lunch, 2 servings of black bean-quinoa Buddha bowl for dinner, 2 glasses of chocolate protein shake, and 4 cups of air-popped popcorns as a snack

- Day 2 – have 2 servings of breakfast oats and quinoa with fruits for breakfast, 2 servings of vegetable burger with broccoli and squash for lunch, 2 glasses of chocolate protein shake, 1/2 cup pumpkin seeds
- Day 3 – have 2 servings of pancakes with berries for breakfast, 2 servings of black bean-quinoa Buddha bowl for dinner, ½ cup pumpkin seeds, and 3 servings of air-popped popcorn as a snack
- Day 4 – have 2 servings of breakfast oats and quinoa with fruits for breakfast, 2 servings of vegetable burger with broccoli and squash for lunch, 2 servings of white bean sandwich with kale for dinner, and 2 servings of air-popped popcorns as a snack
- Day 5 – have 2 servings of pancakes with berries for breakfast, 2 servings of black bean-quinoa Buddha bowl for dinner, 2 glasses of chocolate protein shake, and ½ cup pumpkin seeds as a snack
- Day 6 – have 2 servings of black bean-quinoa Buddha bowl for lunch, 2 servings of vegetable burger with broccoli and squash for dinner, ½ cup pumpkin seeds, and 4 cups air-popped popcorns as a snack

WEEK 3 RECIPES

PANCAKES WITH BERRIES

Serves: 6 pancakes, 2 pancakes, ¼ cup berries, and 1 tablespoon peanut butter per serving
Total Time: 30 minutes
Prep Time: 20 minutes

Tags: low carb, high protein, sugar-free, dairy-free, egg-free, gluten-free

Ingredients:

- 1 ½ cup white whole-wheat flour
- ¼ teaspoon salt
- 2 teaspoons baking powder
- 1 tablespoon sugar
- 1 teaspoon vanilla extract
- 2 tablespoons coconut oil, melted
- 1 ½ cups almond milk, unsweetened
- ¼ cup applesauce, unsweetened
- 2 cups blackberries, fresh
- 4 tablespoons peanut butter

Directions:

1. Take a large bowl, place flour in it, add salt and baking powder and then stir until mixed.
2. Add vanilla, sugar, and oil, pour in the applesauce and milk and then whisk until combined.
3. Gradually whisk flour mixture into the applesauce mixture until incorporated, and then let the batter rest for 15 minutes.
4. When ready to cook, take a large skillet pan, place it over medium heat and then spray it with oil.
5. Ladle ¼ cup of the prepared batter into the pan, cook it for 2 to 4 minutes per side until golden brown and cooked and then transfer the pancake to a plate.
6. Repeat with the remaining batter, cook five more pancakes and then let them cool completely.
7. Then place two pancakes into each of three meal prep containers, add ¼ cup blackberries into each container, cover with the lid, and store in the refrigerator for up to 6 days.

8. Spoon peanut butter in a separate mini meal-prep container and store until required.

Nutritional Values per Serving

Calories: 228.8 kcal
Carbohydrates: 26.8 g
Dietary Fiber: 16.3 g
Protein: 9.5 g
Fat: 8.7 g
Saturated Fat: 4.6 g

2

BREAKFAST OATS AND QUINOA WITH FRUITS

Serves: 3 bowls, 1 bowl per serving
Total Time: 40 minutes
Prep Time: 25 minutes

Tags: low carb, high protein, dairy-free, egg-free, sugar-free, gluten-free, coconut-free

Ingredients:

- ¾ cup diced peaches, fresh
- ¾ of a large banana, peeled, mashed
- ¾ cup blueberries, fresh
- ¾ cup rolled oats
- ¾ cup raspberries, fresh
- 3 tablespoons ground flaxseed
- ¼ cup quinoa, rinsed
- 6 tablespoons vanilla-flavored protein powder
- 3 teaspoons ground cinnamon
- 3 teaspoons honey
- 1 teaspoon olive oil
- ½ cup of water
- 2 ¼ cups almond milk, unsweetened

Directions:

1. Cook quinoa, and for this, take a small saucepan, place it over medium-high heat, add oil and then let it heat.
2. Add quinoa, stir until mixed, and then cook for 2 minutes until toasted.
3. Pour in the water, bring the quinoa to a rolling boil, switch heat to the low level, and then continue cooking the quinoa for 10 to 12 minutes, covering the pan with its lid.
4. When done, remove the saucepan from heat, let the quinoa rest for 5 minutes and then fluff it with a fork.
5. Transfer the quinoa into a large bowl, let it cool for 15 minutes, add oats, cinnamon, flax, and protein powder, and then stir until combined.

6. Mash the banana, add to the quinoa bowl, add peaches, berries, and honey, pour in the milk, and then stir until well combined.

7. Distribute quinoa evenly among three meal prep containers, cover with the lid, and then store in the refrigerator for up to 6 days.

Nutritional Values per Serving

Calories: 232 kcal
Carbohydrates: 31.2 g
Dietary Fiber: 20.4 g
Protein: 15.2 g
Fat: 4.8 g
Saturated Fat: 1.2 g

3

WHITE BEAN SANDWICH WITH KALE

Serves: 4 sandwiches, 1 sandwich per serving
Total Time: 25 minutes
Prep Time: 13 minutes
Tags: low carb, high protein, dairy-free, egg-free, gluten-free, coconut-free, sugar-free

Ingredients:

For the Kale:

- 2 large bunches of kale, fresh
- ¼ teaspoon salt
- 1/8 teaspoon red chili flakes
- 2 tablespoons olive oil

For the White Beans:

- 8 ounces canned white beans, drained, rinsed
- ¼ teaspoon minced garlic
- ½ teaspoon salt
- ¼ teaspoon ground black pepper
- 2 tablespoons lemon juice
- 1/8 teaspoon paprika

For the Sandwich:

- 8 slices of whole-wheat bread
- 4 cups sliced cucumber

Directions:

1. Prepare the kale and for this, switch on the oven, then set it to 400 degrees F and let it preheat.
2. Meanwhile, remove the stems of kale, tear its leaves, and then place them in a large bowl.
3. Drizzle oil over the kale, sprinkle with salt and red chili flakes, and then toss until coated.
4. Take two large baking sheets, line them with parchment sheets, spread kale leaves in a single layer on them, and then roast for 10 to 12 minutes until roasted and slightly crisp, tossing halfway.

5. Meanwhile, place white beans in a food processor, add salt, black pepper, garlic, and lemon juice, and then pulse until mixture resembles a chunky paste.

6. Toast the bread slices until golden brown on all sides and then arrange them on a clean working space.

7. Spread the bean mixture evenly on top of four bread slices, top with roasted kale leaves, and then cover with the remaining bread slices.

8. Wrap each sandwich with foil, place each sandwich into four meal prep containers, and add 1 cup cucumber slices into each meal prep container.

9. Cover the meal prep containers with each of their lids and then store them for up to 6 days.

Nutritional Values per Serving

Calories: 332.8 kcal
Carbohydrates: 46.6 g
Dietary Fiber: 29.5 g
Protein: 15.1 g
Fat: 9.5 g
Saturated Fat: 1.6 g

4

VEGETABLE BURGER WITH BROCCOLI AND SQUASH

Serves: 4 burgers, 1 burger, ½ cup broccoli florets and ¾ cup squash pieces per serving
Total Time: 45 minutes
Prep Time: 15 minutes

Tags: low carb, high protein, dairy-free, egg-free, soy-free, gluten-free, sugar-free

Ingredients:

- 1 cup canned chickpeas
- 2 cups broccoli florets
- 8 ounces frozen mixed vegetables, thawed
- 3 cups cubes of squash
- 2 teaspoons garlic powder
- 4 tablespoons chickpea flour
- 3 teaspoons flaxseed
- 3 teaspoons salt
- 3 teaspoons ground black pepper
- 6 tablespoons olive oil
- 4 tablespoons water
- 4 whole-wheat burger bun

Directions:

1. Switch on the oven, then set it to 450 degrees F and let it preheat.
2. Meanwhile, take a large bowl, place broccoli florets, and then sprinkle with 1 teaspoon garlic powder and 1 teaspoon each of salt and black pepper.
3. Drizzle 2 tablespoons oil over the broccoli florets, and then toss until coated.
4. Take a large bowl, place the squash pieces in it, and then sprinkle with 1 teaspoon garlic powder and 1 teaspoon each of salt and black pepper.
5. Drizzle 2 tablespoons oil over the squash pieces and then toss until coated.
6. Take a baking sheet, spread broccoli florets on it in a single

layer and then bake for 20 minutes until roasted and tender-crisp, tossing halfway.

7. Take a separate baking sheet, spread the squash pieces on it in a single layer, and then bake for 20 minutes until golden brown and tender, tossing halfway.

8. Meanwhile, prepare the vegetable patties and for this, take a small bowl, place flaxseed in it, stir in water, and let it rest for 5 minutes.

9. Pour the flaxseed mixture into the food processor, add chickpeas and vegetables in a food processor, add chickpea flour and remaining salt and black pepper, and then pulse until just mixed.

10. Tip the mixture into a bowl and then shape the mixture into four patties.

11. Take a large skillet pan, place it over medium-high heat, add remaining oil and when hot, add patties in it and then cook for 3 to 5 minutes per side until golden brown and crisp.

12. When done, transfer chickpeas patties to a plate and let them cool completely.

13. Meanwhile, transfer roasted broccoli florets and squash pieces to a separate plate and let them cool completely.

14. Cut the burger buns in half, toast them, and then sandwich chickpea patties between them.

15. Place a vegetable burger into each of the four meal prep containers, evenly add broccoli florets and squash pieces, and then cover the containers with the lid.

16. Store the meal prep containers in the refrigerator for up to 6 days.

Nutritional Values Per Serving

Calories: 312 kcal

Carbohydrates: 51.5 g
Dietary Fiber: 35.5 g
Protein: 12.5 g
Fat: 6.2 g
Saturated Fat: 0.8 g

5

BLACK BEAN-QUINOA BUDDHA BOWL

Serves: 4 bowls, 1 bowl per serving
Total Time: 1 hour
Prep Time: 15 minutes

Tags: low carb, high protein, dairy-free, egg-free, gluten-free, sugar-free, coconut-free

Ingredients:

- 1 medium avocado, diced
- 3 cups canned black beans, drained, rinsed
- 2 cups quinoa, rinsed
- 4 tablespoons lime juice
- 12 tablespoons pico de gallo
- 1 cup hummus
- 3 ½ cups water
- 8 tablespoons chopped cilantro, fresh

For the Hummus:

- 1 cup canned chickpeas
- ½ of lemon, juiced
- 1 tablespoon olive oil
- 1 clove of garlic, peeled
- ¼ teaspoon ground cumin
- ¼ teaspoon salt

For the pico de gallo:

- ¼ of a medium white onion, peeled, diced
- 4 medium tomatoes, diced
- 1 medium jalapeno pepper, minced
- 1 teaspoon minced garlic
- 1/3 teaspoon salt
- 1 tablespoon lime juice
- ¼ cup minced cilantro

Directions:

1. Cook quinoa, and for this, take a large saucepan, place it over medium-high heat, add oil and then let it heat.
2. Add quinoa, stir until mixed, and then cook for 5 minutes until toasted.
3. Pour in the water, bring the quinoa to a rolling boil, then switch heat to the low level and continue cooking the quinoa for 25 to 30 minutes, covering the pan with its lid.
4. When done, remove the saucepan from heat, let the quinoa rest for 5 minutes and then fluff it with a fork.
5. Transfer the quinoa into a large bowl, let it cool for 15 minutes, add black beans and then stir until combined.
6. Divide the quinoa-bean mixture evenly among four meal prep containers, cover the containers with its lid, and store in the refrigerator for up to 6 days.
7. Prepare the hummus and for this, place all of its ingredients in a food processor and then pulse until smooth.
8. Tip the hummus in a medium bowl, add lime juice in it, and then stir until combined.
9. Store the hummus mixture in a separate meal prep container and then store it until required.
10. Prepare the pico de gallo and for this, take a medium bowl, place all of its ingredients in it and then stir until mixed.
11. Store the pico de gallo in a separate meal prep container and then store it until required.
12. Store the avocado separately until required.
13. When ready to eat, drizzle the hummus mixture over the quinoa-bean mixture, and then drizzle the pico de gallo.
14. Dice the avocado, top the avocado pieces over the black bean and quinoa, sprinkle cilantro on top, and then serve.

Nutritional Values Per Serving

Calories: 320 kcal
Carbohydrates: 46 g
Dietary Fiber: 31.6 g
Protein: 15.7 g
Fat: 8.1 g
Saturated Fat: 1.5 g

CHOCOLATE PROTEIN SHAKE

Serves: 4 jars, 1 jar per serving
Total Time: 5 minutes
Prep Time: 5 minutes
Tags: low carb, high protein, soy-free, gluten-free, sugar-free

Ingredients:

- 1 ¼ cups chocolate-flavored protein powder
- 8 tablespoons peanut powder
- 4 tablespoons MCT oil
- 4 cups almond milk, unsweetened
- 2 cups of ice cubes

Directions:

1. Take three Mason jars, add ¼ cup and 2 tablespoons protein powder, 1 tablespoon MCT oil, 2 tablespoons peanut powder, and then pour in 1 cup milk.
2. Shut the jars with its lid, store them in the refrigerator for up to 6 days and when ready to drink, uncover a jar and pour in ½ cup ice cubes and then puree by using an immersion blender until smooth.

Nutritional Values Per Serving

Calories: 150.4 kcal
Carbohydrates: 8.8 g
Dietary Fiber: 4.6 g
Protein: 15.9 g
Fat: 5.6 g
Saturated Fat: 0.8 g

And then I realized
that to be
more alive
I had to
be less
afraid
so
I did it...
I lost my
fear
and gained
my whole life.

WEEK 4

BEFORE WE MOVE ON...

Hi there!

How do you feel about the meal prep for the first 3 weeks? Do you like it? I personally love Tofu scramble in week 2! It's easy to prepare and healthy to eat, and it looks so beautiful!

Before we start week 4, I'd like to ask you for a favor.

As you know, my wife & I put quite a lot of effort to develop our own set of vegan recipes and realized that this might be helpful for some people who are struggling to prep their plant-based meals. We do everything that we can to make sure that all recipes are healthy and delicious.

If you find the recipes and meal plan helpful, would you kindly help us by leaving a brief review to share your experience? (Just 1 or 2 sentences will help a lot!)

As an indie author, reviews don't come easily and they are the biggest motivation for me and my wife to keep going. It will take you a few seconds, but it will literally make our day!

If you would like to give us a big hand and post your review now, please go to: shorturl.at/gzGNP.

Thank you for your support. Now, let's move on to the final week of meal prepping, shall we?

Best Regards,

Benjamin

WEEK 4 MEAL PREP GUIDE

Week 4 - Menu

Breakfast:
Vanilla Breakfast Protein Bites
Blueberry Banana Rice Cake Mousse

Lunch & Dinner:
Red Cabbage and Walnuts Salad
Potato Stew with Green Beans and Roasted Peanuts
Cauliflower with White Beans and Tomato Sauce

Snacks:
Kale Chips
Goji Berries
Cashews

WEEK 4 MEAL PLAN

YOUR HEALTHY MEAL PLAN

MONDAY

Breakfast: Vanilla Breakfast Protein Bites
Snack: Cashews
Lunch: Red Cabbage and Walnuts Salad
Snack: Kale Chips
Dinner: Cauliflower with White Beans and
Tomato Sauce

Calories: 1138
Carbohydrates: 117.4
Dietary Fiber: 72.4
Protein: 65.8
Fat: 44.5
Saturated Fat: 15.2
Net Carb: 45

TUESDAY

Breakfast: Blueberry Banana Rice Cake Mousse
Snack: Kale Chips
Lunch: Potato Stew with Green Beans and
Roasted Peanuts
Snack: Goji Berries
Dinner: Red Cabbage and Walnuts Salad

Calories: 1167
Carbohydrates: 109.4
Dietary Fiber: 62.3
Protein: 48.9
Fat: 57.5
Saturated Fat: 18.7
Net Carb: 47.1

WEDNESDAY

Breakfast: Vanilla Breakfast Protein Bites
Snack: Cashews
Lunch: Red Cabbage and Walnuts Salad
Snack: Goji Berries
Dinner: Cauliflower with White Beans and
Tomato Sauce

Calories: 1184
Carbohydrates: 121
Dietary Fiber: 72.7
Protein: 63.9
Fat: 50
Saturated Fat: 15.2
Net Carb: 48.2

THURSDAY

Breakfast: Blueberry Banana Rice Cake Mousse
Snack: Kale Chips
Lunch: Potato Stew with Green Beans and
Roasted Peanuts
Snack: Cashews
Dinner: Red Cabbage and Walnuts Salad

Calories: 1172
Carbohydrates: 120.4
Dietary Fiber: 70.1
Protein: 54.4
Fat: 49.7
Saturated Fat: 16.9
Net Carb: 50.3

FRIDAY

Breakfast: Vanilla Breakfast Protein Bites
Snack: Goji Berries
Lunch: Potato Stew with Green Beans and
Roasted Peanuts
Snack: Kale Chips
Dinner: Cauliflower with White Beans and
Tomato Sauce

Calories: 1174
Carbohydrates: 125.2
Dietary Fiber: 74.8
Protein: 64.7
Fat: 44.33
Saturated Fat: 12.4
Net Carb: 50.4

SATURDAY

Breakfast: Blueberry Banana Rice Cake
Mousse
Snack: Cashews
Lunch: Cauliflower with White Beans and
Tomato Sauce
Snack: Goji Berries
Dinner: Potato Stew with Green Beans and
Roasted Peanuts

Calories: 1214
Carbohydrates: 139.2
Dietary Fiber: 82.3
Protein: 67.3
Fat: 41.4
Saturated Fat: 10.5
Net Carb: 56.9

2

WEEK 4 - SHOPPING LIST

WEEK 4 SHOPPING LIST

YOUR HEALTHY MEAL PREPARATION

Pantry Items

- [ ] 2 ½ tablespoons cinnamon
- [ ] 1 tablespoon paprika
- [ ] 2 ½ tablespoons vanilla extract
- [ ] 2 tablespoons and 1 teaspoon apple cider vinegar
- [ ] ¼ cup marinara sauce

Vegetables and Fruits

- [ ] 1 ½ medium banana
- [ ] ¾ cup fresh blueberries
- [ ] 4 medium apples
- [ ] 2 cups goji berries
- [ ] 6 cups shredded red cabbage
- [ ] 8 cups cauliflower florets
- [ ] 1 large white onion
- [ ] 32 grape tomatoes
- [ ] 16 ounces potatoes
- [ ] 1 pound curly kale
- [ ] 24 ounces green beans
- [ ] 2 medium cucumber
- [ ] 1 1/3 cup spinach leaves
- [ ] 2 teaspoons minced garlic
- [ ] 12 tablespoons sliced basil
- [ ] 6 cups vegetable broth

Protein

- [ ] 4 2/3 cups almond milk
- [ ] 4 ½ tablespoons and 1 1/3 cup vanilla protein powder
- [ ] ¼ cup protein powder, unflavored
- [ ] ¼ cup grated parmesan cheese, vegan

Beans, Legumes, Grains

- [ ] 2 cups canned white beans
- [ ] 2 cups canned chickpeas
- [ ] 3 2/3 cups porridge oats
- [ ] 5 rice cakes

Nuts, Seeds

- [ ] 13 tablespoons chia seeds
- [ ] 2 ½ cups almond flour
- [ ] 7 tablespoons peanut butter
- [ ] 1 cup crushed walnuts
- [ ] 4 tablespoons roasted peanuts
- [ ] 52 cashews

3

WEEK 4 - MEAL PREP DAY GUIDE

- Step 1: Go through all the recipes for week 4, and prepare all the ingredients that you need.
- Step 2: Switch on the oven, set it to 325 degrees F for the kale chips, and let it preheat.
- Step 3: Prepare the chia mix of Vanilla Breakfast Protein Bites and let it sit for 10 minutes.
- Step 4: Prepare the mousse of Blueberry Banana Rice Cake Mousse and then store it.
- Step 5: Assemble the ingredients for the bite mix of Vanilla Breakfast Protein Bites, prepare the protein bites, and store them.
- Step 6: Gather the ingredients of Red Cabbage and Walnuts Salad, assemble the salad and store it.
- Step 7: Gather the ingredients for the Potato Stew with Green Beans and Roasted Peanuts, cook it, and then let it cool completely.
- Step 8: Prepare the kale chips, bake them, and let them cool completely.
- Step 9: Boil the florets of Cauliflower with White Beans and Tomato Sauce and then let them cool completely.

- Step 10: Cook the white beans and tomato sauce for the Cauliflower with White Beans and Tomato Sauce and then cool it completely.
- Step 11: Assemble the meal prep containers for the Potato Stew with Green Beans and Roasted Peanuts and store them.
- Step 12: Assemble the salad in the recipe of Potato Stew with Green Beans and Roasted Peanuts and then store it.
- Step 13: Assemble the meal prep containers for the Cauliflower with White Beans and Tomato Sauce and store them.

When ready to eat:

Vanilla Breakfast Protein Bites – bring the protein bites at room temperature and then serve.

Blueberry Banana Rice Cake Mousse – bring the mousse at room temperature, stir the berries until evenly mixed, and then serve.

Red Cabbage and Walnuts Salad – bring the salad at room temperature and then enjoy it.

Potato Stew with Green Beans and Roasted Peanuts – reheat the container of stew in the microwave for 1 to 2 minutes until hot, bring the chickpea salad to room temperature and then serve.

Cauliflower with White Beans and Tomato Sauce – reheat the container of cauliflower with white beans and tomato sauce in the microwave for 1 to 2 minutes until hot and then serve.

Kale Chips – enjoy straight away as a snack.

Goji Berries – eat ¼ cup of berries as a snack.

Cashews – eat 13 whole cashews as a snack.

· · ·

Modifications

1500 calories

- Day 1 – have 2 servings of red cabbage and walnuts salad for lunch and 2 servings of kale chips as a snack
- Day 2 – have 2 servings of red cabbage and walnuts salad for dinner
- Day 3 – have 2 servings of vanilla breakfast protein bites for breakfast and 19 cashews as a snack
- Day 4 – have 2 servings of red cabbage and walnuts salad for dinner
- Day 5 – have 2 servings of vanilla breakfast protein bites for breakfast and 2 servings of kale chips as a snack
- Day 6 – have 2 servings of blueberry banana rice cake mousse for breakfast

2000 calories

- Day 1 – have 2 servings of red cabbage and walnuts salad for lunch, 2 servings of cauliflower with white beans and tomato sauce for dinner, 2 servings of kale chips, and 26 cashews as a snack
- Day 2 – have 2 servings of blueberry banana rice cake mousse for breakfast, 2 servings of potato stew with green beans and roasted peanuts for lunch, 2 servings of kale chips, and ½ cup goji berries as a snack
- Day 3 – have 2 servings of vanilla breakfast protein bites for breakfast, 2 servings of red cabbage and walnuts salad for lunch, ¼ cup goji berries, and 26 cashews as a snack
- Day 4 – have 2 servings of potato stew with green beans and

roasted peanuts for lunch, 2 servings of red cabbage and walnuts salad for dinner, and 26 cashews as a snack

- Day 5 – have 2 servings of potato stew with green beans and roasted peanuts for lunch, 2 servings of cauliflower with white beans and tomato sauce for dinner, and ½ cup goji berries as a snack
- Day 6 – have 2 servings of blueberry banana rice cake mousse for breakfast, 2 servings of potato stew with green beans and roasted peanuts for dinner, and ½ cup goji berries as a snack

WEEK 4 RECIPES

VANILLA BREAKFAST PROTEIN BITES

Serves: 12 balls, 4 balls per serving
Total Time: 15 minutes
Prep Time: 15 minutes
Tags: low carb, high protein, sugar-free, dairy-free, egg-free, gluten-free

Ingredients:

For the Chia Mix:

- 10 tablespoons chia seeds

- 10 tablespoons almond milk, unsweetened

For the Bite Mix:

- 2 ½ cups almond flour
- 3 2/3 cups porridge oats
- 2 ½ tablespoon ground cinnamon
- 1 1/3 cup vanilla protein powder
- 2 ½ tablespoons vanilla extract, unsweetened
- 2 ½ cups almond milk, unsweetened

Directions:

1. Place the chia seeds in a small bowl, pour in the milk, stir until just mixed, and then let it sit for 10 minutes.
2. Transfer the porridge oats to a food processor and then pulse until the mixture resembles flour.
3. Tip the oat flour in a bowl, add almond flour, cinnamon, and protein powder, and then stir until mixed.
4. Pour in vanilla and milk and then whisk until smooth batter comes together.
5. Add the chia seeds mixture, stir until mixed, and then shape the mixture into twenty-four balls.
6. Then divide the balls into three meal prep containers, cover with the lid, and store in the refrigerator for up to 6 days.

Nutritional Values per Serving

Calories: 263 kcal
Carbohydrates: 24 g
Dietary Fiber: 15 g
Protein: 17 g
Fat: 11 g
Saturated Fat: 3 g

BLUEBERRY BANANA RICE CAKE MOUSSE

Serves: 3 jars, 1 jar per serving
Total Time: 15 minutes
Prep Time: 15 minutes
Tags: low carb, high protein, sugar-free, dairy-free, egg-free, gluten-free

Ingredients:

- 1 ½ cup almond milk, unsweetened
- 1 ½ of a medium banana
- ¾ cup fresh blueberries
- 3 tablespoons chia seeds
- 3 tablespoons peanut butter
- 3 rice cakes, crumbled
- 4 ½ tablespoons vanilla flavored protein powder

Directions:

1. Place all the ingredients in a food processor, reserving the berries, and then pulse until blended.
2. Divide the mousse evenly among three mason jars, and then top with ¼ cup berries.
3. Cover the jars with the lid and then store in the refrigerator for up to 6 days.

Nutritional Values per Serving

Calories: 252 kcal
Carbohydrates: 23.4 g
Dietary Fiber: 14.4 g
Protein: 16 g
Fat: 10.4 g
Saturated Fat: 2.9 g

3

RED CABBAGE AND WALNUTS SALAD

Serves: 4 bowls, 1 bowl per serving
Total Time: 15 minutes
Prep Time: 15 minutes
Tags: low carb, high protein, sugar-free, dairy-free, egg-free, gluten-free

Ingredients:

- 4 medium apples, cored, sliced
- 6 cups shredded red cabbage
- 4 medium scallion, sliced
- 1 cup crushed walnuts
- 1 1/3 teaspoon sea salt
- 2 tablespoons apple cider vinegar
- 2 tablespoons olive oil

Directions:

1. Take a large bowl, place apple slices in it, and then add shredded cabbage.
2. Drizzle oil over the apple and cabbage, drizzle with vinegar, toss until coated, and then season with salt.
3. Divide the salad evenly among four meal prep containers, top with ¼ cup of walnuts, cover with the lid, and store in the refrigerator for up to 6 days.

Nutritional Values per Serving

Calories: 343 kcal
Carbohydrates: 28.8 g
Dietary Fiber: 17.1 g
Protein: 10.2 g
Fat: 20.8 g
Saturated Fat: 8.4 g

4

POTATO STEW WITH GREEN BEANS AND ROASTED PEANUTS

Serves: 4 bowls, 1 bowl per serving
Total Time: 45 minutes
Prep Time: 15 minutes
Tags: low carb, high protein, sugar-free, dairy-free, egg-free, gluten-free

Ingredients:

For the Stew:

- 1 large white onion, peeled, chopped
- 16 ounces potatoes, peeled, diced
- 24 ounces green beans
- 2 teaspoons minced garlic
- 2 teaspoons salt
- 1 teaspoon ground black pepper
- 3 tablespoons olive oil
- 6 cups vegetable broth

For the Topping:

- 4 tablespoons roasted peanut

For the Salad:

- 2 cups cooked chickpeas
- 32 grape tomatoes
- 2 medium cucumbers, chopped
- 1 1/3 cup spinach leaves, fresh
- 1 tablespoon smoked paprika
- 1 teaspoon of sea salt
- 1 tablespoon olive oil

Directions:

1. Take a large pot, place it over medium heat, add oil, and then let it heat.

2. Add onion, stir until coated in oil, and then cook for 8 to 10 minutes until tender and golden brown.

3. Add garlic into the pot, stir until mixed, and then cook for 1 minute until fragrant.

4. Add potatoes, season with salt and black pepper, pour in the vegetable broth, and then bring the mixture to a boil.

5. Remove pot from heat and then puree the stew by using an immersion blender until smooth.

6. Add green beans into the pot, return the pot over medium heat, cook the beans for 10 minutes until tender, and then let the stew cool completely.

7. Prepare the salad and for this, take a large bowl, add all the ingredients in it and then toss until mixed.

8. Ladle the stew evenly into four meal prep containers, sprinkle 1 tablespoon of peanuts on top, cover with the lid, and store in the refrigerator for up to 6 days.

9. Divide the salad evenly among four mini meal prep containers, cover with the lid, and store in the refrigerator for up to 6 days.

Nutritional Values per Serving

Calories: 384 kcal
Carbohydrates: 47.6 g
Dietary Fiber: 27.3 g
Protein: 14.6 g
Fat: 12.8 g
Saturated Fat: 3.8 g

CAULIFLOWER WITH WHITE BEANS AND TOMATO SAUCE

Serves: 4 plates, 1 plate per serving
Total Time: 30 minutes
Prep Time: 10 minutes
Tags: low carb, high protein, sugar-free, dairy-free, egg-free, gluten-free

Ingredients:

- 8 cups cauliflower florets
- 2 cups canned white beans
- 2 cups crushed tomato
- 2 teaspoons salt
- 12 tablespoons fresh basil, sliced
- 4 tablespoons peanut butter

Directions:

1. Take a large pot, fill it half with water, place it over medium-high heat and then bring it to a boil.
2. Add cauliflower florets, boil the florets for 5 to 10 minutes until tender, drain the florets, and then cool completely.
3. Drain the pot, place it over medium-high heat, add butter, white beans, tomatoes, and salt, stir until mixed, and then simmer for 1 to 2 minutes until thoroughly hot.
4. When done, remove the pot from heat and then let it cool completely.
5. Divide the cooled cauliflower florets evenly among four meal prep containers, ladle white beans and tomato sauce over the florets, cover with the lid, and store in the refrigerator for up to 6 days.

Nutritional Values per Serving

Calories: 339 kcal
Carbohydrates: 44 g
Dietary Fiber: 29 g
Protein: 25 g
Fat: 7 g
Saturated Fat: 2 g

KALE CHIPS

Serves: 4 portions, 1 portion per serving
Total Time: 1 hour and 10 minutes
Prep Time: 10 minutes
Tags: low carb, high protein, soy-free, gluten-free, sugar-free

Ingredients:

- 1 pound curly kale
- ½ teaspoon of sea salt
- ¼ cup protein powder, unflavored
- 2 tablespoons olive oil
- 1 teaspoon apple cider vinegar
- ¼ cup marinara sauce
- ¼ cup grated parmesan cheese, vegan

Directions:

1. Switch on the oven, then set it to 325 degrees F and let it preheat.
2. Rinse the kale, pat dry, remove the stem and then tear the leaves into bite-size pieces.
3. Take a large bowl, add protein powder, salt, and cheese, pour in marinara sauce, vinegar and oil and then whisk until smooth.
4. Add kale leaves pieces to the marinara sauce mixture, and then toss until well coated.
5. Take two large baking sheets, line them with parchment sheets, spread the kale evenly between the baking sheets, and then bake for 30 minutes per side until crisp, turning halfway.
6. Let the kale leaves cool completely, divide evenly among four meal prep bags, seal tightly and then store at room temperature.

Nutritional Values per Serving

Calories: 71 kcal
Carbohydrates: 3 g
Dietary Fiber: 1.6 g
Protein: 5 g
Fat: 4 g
Saturated Fat: 1.8 g

WHEN YOU
FEEL LIKE
QUITTING,
THINK ABOUT
WHY YOU
STARTED

Hey guys!

I've created a group where members from different parts of the world can talk about health, food, fitness, and other related stuff!

We can all share our recipes, workout routines, or even ask for tips and advices. Sounds cool?

Be part of our growing plant-based community today!

www.facebook.com/groups/veganrecipesandsupport

CONCLUSION

First of all, I want to say a big thank you to you for sticking with this for the last 28 days. I know that it has been difficult and that you have probably wanted to give up and return to eating all the typical things that you love so much. Perhaps you even had a little cheat meal here or there. The important thing to remember is that making a commitment to your health is about taking baby steps in the right direction.

That you have made it to the end of the 28 day plan is testament to your commitment to a new way of life. That might sound like an exaggeration, but it really is not. You have entirely changed the way you eat and live in the space of 28 days. That is less than a month. You ought to be proud of yourself, I know that I am very happy that you have made it this far and that you have stuck to the plan. If it is your first run through the 28 days plan then you might not feel the change yet, but trust me, the vegan diet is already working wonders for you on the inside. This plan can be repeated again and again; also use it as a guide to create your own meal plan with your own favorite high-protein plant-based meals.

It can be difficult to believe in yourself, but I believe in you, just like I believe in each person who walks into my gym and tells me they want a better, fitter, healthier life. Why do I believe in them? Because they, just like you, have already made the first step. They literally step into the gym. In this case you have bought this book. Self belief is not always in plentiful supply particularly when it comes to getting fit and building muscle.

Before you know it you will have month after month of healthy eating under your belt and it will no longer be something you need to consciously think about doing. It will just be a habit that will not be difficult to maintain. As you have discovered over the last 28 days, healthy plant-based food is bursting with fresh flavors, tantalizing textures, and glorious goodness. You do not need to eat a lot to feel full, but what you do eat will be packed full of nutrition, vitamins and all the good stuff that keeps your body healthy and fit.

ACKNOWLEDGMENTS

Thank you, Trisha, for always being there and supporting me and our daughter. I couldn't have done it without you.

Thank you, readers, for taking the time to read our book. It's our mission to continuously create delicious and healthy recipes to help more people transition into a plant-based diet and be able to live a happier, healthier lifestyle.

If you have enjoyed this book, it will mean the world to us if you could take a few seconds to **write a review on Amazon**. Just one or two words will help us indie authors tremendously and I will be eternally grateful.

Go here now to post your review: shorturl.at/gzGNP

Keep smiling, and keep being the strong, kind and amazing human being that you are.

Much love,

Benjamin

Made in the USA
Las Vegas, NV
05 May 2024

89497599R00109